IF I HAD A HAMMER

WOMEN'S WORK

In Poetry, Fiction, and Photographs

IF I HAD A HAMMER
WOMEN'S WORK

In Poetry, Fiction, and Photographs

Edited by Sandra Martz

Papier-Mache Press - Watsonville, California

First Edition.

93 92 91   8 7 6 5 4

ISBN: 0-918949-09-2

Editorial assistance provided by Roberta Goodwin and Dina Nocente.
Cover art, "Still Life with Workers," © 1990 by Victoria Hamlin, photographed by Ken Rice.

Grateful acknowledgement is made as follows: *Times Monitor*, for "Teaching" by Katharyn Machan Aal; Borealis Press Limited for "Piece Work" by Mona Elaine Adilman; *Z Miscellaneous* for "Quilting" by Meleta Murdock Baker; *New Voices 64* (MacMillan Company) for "Hands" by Mildred Barker; *Room of One's Own* for "Girl on the Crew" and "These Hips" by Kate Braid; *Woman Sitting at the Machine, Thinking* (Red Letter Press) for the excerpt from "Woman Sitting at the Machine, Thinking" by Karen Brodine; *Iris 21* for "Sprezzatura" by Maxine Combs; *Blue Unicorn* for "Mowing at Dusk" by Barbara Crooker; *Footwork Magazine* for "The Last Woman in America to Wash Diapers" by Barbara Crooker; *Mill Hunk Herald* and *Crossing the Mainstream* (Silverleaf Press, Inc.) for "Cultural Worker" by Sue Doro; *Tradeswomen* for "Definitions" by Sue Doro; *Bay Windows* for "About Cleaning Bathrooms" by Kathryn Eberly; *It's a Good Thing I'm Not Macho* (Whetstone) for "Through the Ceiling, Maiden Voyage" by Susan Eisenberg; *The Laurel Review* and *Living Inland* (Bennington Press) for "I'm Standing in Line" by Rina Ferrarelli; *Woodwriter Magazine* for "Diana the Good" by Kathy Freeperson; *The Tribe of Dina* (Sinister Wisdom Books) for "How Is This Week Different?" by Ellen Gruber Garvey; *The Pacific Review* for "Blanca Cats" by Penny Gasaway; *Kalliope* for "Handmade Book" by Elizabeth Gilliland; Andrew Mountain Press for "Sabbath Macaroons" by Bina Goldfield; *Nothing Should Fall to Waste* (Arts Wayland Foundation) for "Two Grey Hills" by Nancy Roxbury Knutson; *Redbook* for "Huevos" by Diane Lefer; *Tradeswomen* for "Sweetheart" by Molly Martin; *Z Miscellaneous* for "Committee Meeting" by Lillian Morrison; *Love Me Like You Mean It* (HerBooks) for "Adjustments" by Lesléa Newman; *Wyoming Writing* for "An Anasazi Woman Speaks" by Ginny Odenbach; *Sou'wester* for "Star" by Jacklyn Potter; *Poets On: Working* for "Las Lechuzas" by Jacklyn Potter; *Now and Then* for "The Runner" by Georgeann Eskievich Rettberg; *Empty Window Review* for "Working the Clay" by Elisavietta Ritchie; *Mill Hunk Herald* for "Marilyn McCusker: Coal Miner" and *Catholic Review* for "Mother Teresa in Calcutta" by Savina A. Roxas; *Stalking the Florida Panther* (The Word Works, Inc.) for "The Tomato Packing Plant Line" by Enid Shomer; *Nassau Review '89* "Found Money" by Patti Tana; *Southern Humanities Review* for "Radium Girls" by Barbara Unger; *The Greenfield Review* for "Women at Thirty" by Michele Wolf.

Library of Congress Cataloging-in-Publication Data

If I had a hammer : women's work in poetry, fiction, and photographs /
    edited by Sandra Martz. — 1st ed.
        p. cm.
    ISBN-0-918949-09-2 : $11.00
    1. Women — Employment — Literary collections. 2. American
literature — Women authors. 3. Women — Employment — Pictorial works.
4. American literature — 20th century. 5. Work — Literary
collections. I. Martz, Sandra. II. Title: Women's work.
PS506.W6I38 1990
810.8'0352042 — dc20
                                                    90-7580
                                                    CIP

To all my sisters, and especially to my dear sisters, Sheila and Sherrie.

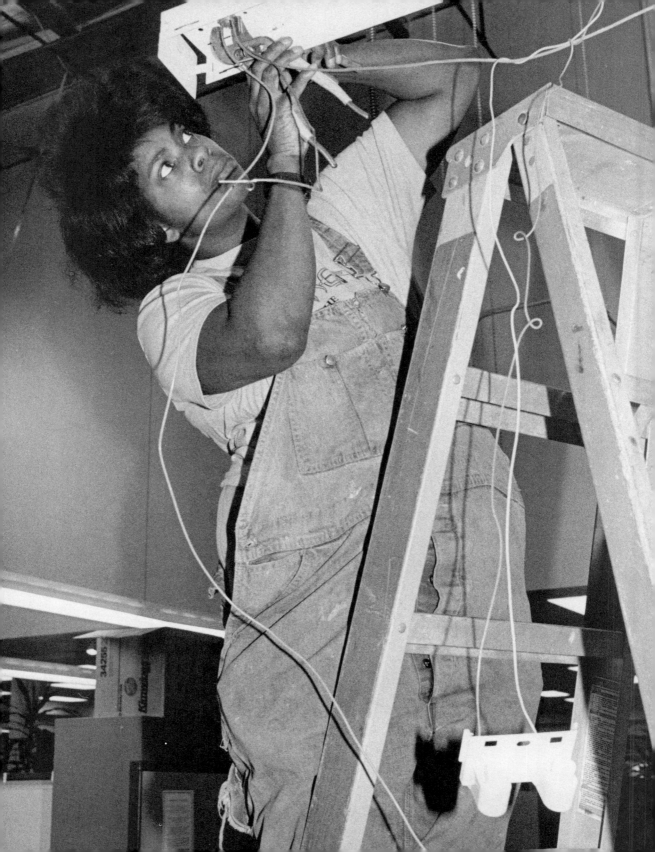

Contents

Photo by Sandy Thacker

"I'm proud of what we've accomplished but all along the way we've had to fight with internalized messages that say you can't do this—you're just a girl!"

—Janice Goldfrank

Foreword

If I Had a Hammer began with a call for material about women and work, a theme broadly defined to encompass unpaid work and activities pursued for creative value, as well as efforts undertaken primarily for money. The result is both literary and documentary, a candid reporting of women's feelings and beliefs about their work.

This collection does not represent all women's work but rather those work experiences women have chosen to write about. I wanted to present as wide an array of occupations as possible and yet many stories go untold. Some professions, areas such as the military, law enforcement, and medicine, seemed especially underrepresented. I wondered why these areas, so filled with human drama and certainly with many stories, produced so few submissions. Perhaps the answer lies in part in this response from Susan Jacobson, a Certified Nursing Assistant.

"Why don't medical people write?" We protect ourselves from knowing what we are doing because it is so devastating: the wounds, cancer, deaths are overwhelming; the stress high; the time, short. We try to be as kind as possible and can't avoid liking or disliking patients. But to go home and think about it is too much (although none of us can avoid that either).

We give the best possible medical care, but in doing so we have divided the patient among us: a leg for the surgeon, pain for the RN, dressings for the LPN, emotions/thoughts for Psych (or the chaplains). I have met people in every position who have awed me with their compassion and caring, but, for the most part, the system militates against anything necessary for the arts.

If I were to choose one word to decribe *If I Had a Hammer*, it would be empowerment. This is not to say that a utopian workplace is portrayed herein. Exploitation has not been eradicated, equal pay is still the goal, not the reality. Work can often be boring and unfulfilling. But the women here are not victims. They set boundaries, draw lines over which they will not cross. They find beauty and art in routine tasks. They take risks, demand respect from coworkers and management, and maintain self-esteem under the most difficult of circumstances. Janice Goldfrank, who owns and operates her own construction firm, describes an important element of women's changing perceptions about their work:

I've been a tradeswoman for about fourteen years. In 1982 I got together with some other women to start our own business. Just women, with no men to teach us or help us. At first we did repairs and small jobs and in seven years we worked up to building houses and doing general contracting. I'm proud of what we accomplished but all along the way we had to fight with internalized messages that said "you can't do this—you're just a girl!" But each new project was bigger than the one before and each success reinforced our belief in ourselves.

After a while I realized that these were skills I could pass on to other women and started teaching workshops. I discovered that the first step is the most profound. Getting over the initial fear of tools and machines spans a giant chasm in our emotional lives. When you do something you've been told all your life that only men can do—it's very powerful. It can transform.

Once women discover they can handle tools, they are ready to believe the rest. They can see that going on to bigger projects is only a matter of degree, of increments of time and experience. The mystique is shattered forever. And when they realize they can do this thing, what else in their lives might work the same way?

In traditional and nontraditional jobs, at home and in the workplace, women are making that discovery. My hope is that these images of women taking charge of their lives will inspire readers to explore, literally and figuratively: What could I do, *If I Had a Hammer.*

—*SANDRA MARTZ*

"And when they realize they can do this thing, what else in their lives might work the same way?"
— Janice Goldfrank

An Anasazi Woman Speaks
Ginny Odenbach

I was here. I came this way.

With the rabbit brush
You dig from your fields
I wove a carrying basket
And worked into it a dark
Design of eagles' claws.
My signature — inked
With sneezeweed dyes.

With the feathers you pluck
From your turkey and burn
I wove a blanket,
A cape to wear when
Winds blow chilly.

With the yucca you ignore
I shod my feet and washed my hair
Weaving sandals from the leaves
And making soapweed suds from the roots.

With the yarrow leaves the wind scatters
I made tea, hot and strong,
To warm and cure and calm.

With the clay beneath your feet
That gumbo which sticks to your boots,
I coiled pots, and mugs,
And sacred feather holders.

With the soft inner bark
Of the juniper, I diapered my baby,
Or crushed it between my hands
To make a nest for the spark
From my fire bow.

I ground red hematite
Between two stones and mixed it
With my honey-colored urine
Then slapped my painty palm
Against the canyon wall, saying,

I was here. I came this way.

The Runner

Georgeann Eskievich Rettberg

On the cellar steps
I was telephone listener
watching rainbows roll into cold water.
White suds turned grey and vanished.
Clean wash rolled into a bushel.

Then — clothes sorter
cotton mounds covered the floor,
whites   colors   railroad   steel mill.
I carried them to grandmother
in the right time and order.

In the morning sun — pin holder
clothes on her shoulders, my mother
held a shirt   six pins   two in her lips,
wooden cigars with no smoke.
We sidestepped across the bricks.
I held two more for the switch in my fist.

Now I'm the runner.
My grandmother in the cellar
magic fingers slip steaming clothes
through the wringer.
I carry the ready bushel to my mother
pass pins   race the empty to the basement
for the next load
crawling through the wringers slit mouth
just in time.

Soon I will guide clean clothes to the bushel
be the clothes shaker   sock hanger
maybe one day   pole heaver
chief hanger   wringer operator
moving up the line
in the business of Monday wash.

Found Money
Patti Tana

Almost every day I find
a penny on the street.
And if the penny faces up
I call it luck.
And if it's down
I call it money.

When I was young
I helped my mom clean a store at night
after her regular job.
I'd spray counters with ammonia
that went up my nose and stung my eyes
then rub away the fingerprints
with a soft cloth.
I'd scrape gum from the floors
and hold the pan as she swept
in dust and black dirt.

Sometimes I'd find coins in the dressing room.
I even found a dollar
behind a row of gowns.
No matter if I found a dollar or a dime
Mom made me leave it with a note
on the big wooden register.

Once I found a wallet
on the floor of a movie theater.
No name.   No pictures.   Only money.
Even in the dark I could see
it was red, smooth plastic red.
I looked at my mother
and she looked away.

Almost everyday I find
a penny on the street.
And if the penny faces up
I call it luck.
And if it's down
I call it money.

6

Sabbath Macaroons
Bina Goldfield

Her cadence whipping egg whites
in the blue-speckled enamel bowl
has the urgent beat of bangles
on a frenzied dancing girl —
As I, the youngest of her daughters, mesmerized
by rising peaks of foam
shell the almonds faster, longing
to brush away the error of flour
from her cheek.

Just in time
the scents of raisin wine, of macaroons dispel
the sour smell of ghetto rancor —
just in time
she lights the candles
that summon Sabbath stars.

Quilting
Meleta Murdock Baker

It occurs to me why I want to make a quilt.
Of course, because Grandma did them, womanbeautiful

but also because my life seems so in pieces
not broken or scattered, but
I'm always working at putting together

fitting schedules and needs
piecing time to personalities
different sizes of energy scraps
various shapes of commitment

Making a cohesive unit
something functional and lovely
It's all done with hidden stitches
sturdy and minute

Photo by Clytia Fuller

Spring Cleaning

Joanne Seltzer

Thanks to my husband I support myself
by caring for an oversize doll house
that I love and hate and wish would collapse
into a heap of building supplies. If

you come up with a better word than housewife,
I'll wear it. In the meantime, call me Ms.
Not Mrs. Haven't I the right to choose
my own name? Though I don't control my life,

allow me at least an identity.
Not Miss.   Not Madam.   Like a ManuScript,
a Motor Ship, a Master of Science

or *memoriae sacrum*: the memory
of a divine but vulnerable spirit
damaged by elbow grease and compliance.

The Last Woman in America to Wash Diapers
Barbara Crooker

The last woman in America to wash diapers
lugs the full pail down to the first floor,
heaves it in the washer, makes it spin its offal load.
How many diapers has she sloshed in the toilet,
how many neatly folded stacks has she raised skyward,
soft white squares of cotton, pieces of cloud,
how many double and triple folds has she pinned
on little bottoms? How many nights
of checking beds did she find those buns
raised in the air, loaves resting on a bakery shelf?
She knows the power of bleach, the benefits of rinsing.
On winter nights, when the snow comes pouring down
in glittery drifts, she sees Ivory Flakes,
their slippery iridescence. When it comes
to dealing with the shit in her life,
nothing else is so simple, so white, so clean.

Photo by Marianne Gontarz

These Hips
Kate Braid

Some hips are made for bearing
children, built like stools
square and easy, right
for the passage of birth.

Others are built like mine.
A child's head might never pass
but load me up with two-by-fours
and watch me
bear.

When the men carry sacks of concrete
they hold them high, like boys.
I bear mine low, like a girl
on small, strong hips
built for the birth
of buildings.

"Girl" on the Crew
Kate Braid

The boys flap heavy leather aprons at me
like housewives scaring crows
from the clean back wash.
    Some aprons.   Some wash.
They think if the leather is tough enough
if the hammer handle piercing it is long enough
I will be overcome with primordial dread
or longing.

They chant construction curses at me:
    Lay 'er down!   *Erect those studs!*
and are alarmed when I learn the words.
They build finely tuned traps, give orders I cannot fill
then puzzle when a few of their own
give me passwords.

I learn the signs of entry,
dropping my hammer into its familiar mouth
as my apron whispers *O-o-o-h Welcome!*

I point my finger and corner posts spring into place
shivering themselves into fertile earth at my command.
The surveyors have never seen such accuracy.

I bite off nails with my teeth
shorten boards with a wave of my hand
pierce them through the dark brown love knots.
They gasp.

14

I squat and the flood of my urine digs
whole drainage systems in an instant.
The boys park their backhoes, call their friends
to come see for themselves or they'd never believe it.

The hairs of my head turn to steel and join boards
tongue-in-groove
like lovers along dark lanes.
Drywall is rustling under cover
eager to slip over the studs at my desire.

When I tire, my breasts grow two cherry trees
that depart my chest
and offer me shade, cool juices
while the others suck bitter beans.

At the end of the day the boys are exhausted
from watching.
They fall at my feet and beg for a body like mine.
I am too busy dancing to notice.

Photo by Sandy Thacker

Through the Ceiling, Maiden Voyage
Susan Eisenberg

Sliding
      under an airduct, then

scrabbling crablike along pipes and crossbars—
      my flashlight breaking
      the darkness, my bodyweight
      placed gingerly (not to fall through)—

I ask the stillness,
has another woman passed
                before me?
to witness this
      pulsation of buildinglife:

arteries of plumbing pipes branch across
electric nervelines sinews of metal
secure airducts
         pumping coolbreath/warmbreath
       to the skeletal
framework of iron beams.

How many times I have passed
under ceilings
      unaware
         unsuspecting.

Diana the Good

Kathy Freeperson

Diana the good
knew how to install brake shoes
and water pumps and change
the oil on every foreign car
ever made
ever so gently she took off
the air filter that looked like it
belonged in a giant cigar
and tuned her engines
revved her motor
padded her shock absorbers
and generally went to drag races.

Diana had learned mechanics
from CETA training before the
Ray-gun administration took
away the aid that the unemployed
needed to be employed and gave
it all to defense.

Diana wondered how could you make
a living from something that
sounded like a little
spoiled boy
game that used to amuse her
brother who died in a dare
jumping off of a building when
he was 15 just so his male friends
would not say he was scared.

Diana the good said he would
never make sense to her
seeing his arms and legs mangled
by the fall had been lesson enough
to avoid star wars.

Photo by Clytia Fuller

Sweetheart
Molly Martin

I was doing pretty good on this new job. See, they didn't want to hire me. Said four foot eleven was too short to be a mechanic. The trucks are put up to a certain height they said and I wasn't tall enough to reach them. But after I complained to Fair Employment, they decided it was okay for me to use a ladder.

So here I am on my little ladder under a diesel changing the oil. The roll-up doors on the garage are all open so I'm kind of on display. And I'm the first woman so I'm a curiosity. They all make detours past the maintenance shop just to see me on my ladder. As if I was a two-headed snake or something. Strange how their minds work. Or they'll come in with some "problem" just to get a look at me. Sometimes they'll walk past and make comments, sort of muttered under their breath, but I know they mean for me to hear. I try not to, though. I concentrate on my work and try to ignore them. They're chicken, anyhow. I say, you don't like somebody, you just tell 'em to their face. I'd have more respect for them if they talked right to me.

One time I thought I heard the word bitch but when I turned around the guy was gone, out the door. Now I don't know if it really happened or if I was just paranoid. I decided it doesn't really matter one way or the other, whether I hear it or not. They're trying to get my goat. They're letting me know they don't want me. Well, you do that to me, it's like waving red in front of a bull. No way am I quitting now. The more they bug me, the harder I dig my heels in. Besides, this is the best money I ever made. Beats waitressing any day.

So anyhow, I'm standing there under this truck and I hear from across the yard kinda sing-song but loud, "Hey sweetheart, how ya doin' today?" I squint out into the sun and see this big old red-faced guy waving his arms at me. His belly looks like a hundred pound sack of flour slung over a farmer's shoulder. His waving arms cause the sack of flour to jiggle and expose a rim of pink flesh above his belt. His head looks like an engine block, hair shaved into a military flat top. He must be a teamster, I think. No neck.

I gotta admit my first impulse was to laugh at this fool. Next I wanted to punch his lights out. Now I know some women don't mind being called sweetheart or honey or any of those sugar-coated names. Men will tell you women think it's a compliment—especially older women. Then they look at me as if I should understand. You know, I'm not that old, but it seems like I hate this name calling more the older I get.

I decided if I ignored this joker maybe he'd get the point and leave me alone. Wouldn't you know, that tactic only encouraged him. Every time he'd see me, he'd yell "Heeeeey sweeeetheart" at the top of his lungs so everyone could hear. One day he came right up and introduced himself, friendly as can be. "Hey," he says, holding out a grimy hand, "I'm Harry. Harry the Hunk they call me." I'm like, is he kidding? Harry the Hunk! Is he putting himself down? I had to hide a smile. I wanted to appear serious, intimidating if possible.

"My name's Bev," I scowled, "and I'd appreciate it if you'd call me that."

"Okay, sweetheart," he leered, and walked away.

Well you can imagine, that got my dander up. I fumed about that all week. It got so every night I'd be beating up Harry the Hunk in my dreams. Now I've never been one to criticize any woman for how she chooses to survive in a job. We each pick our own battles. God knows you can't take on every one that comes along. You'd be wrung out like a dishrag at the end of every day. Some insults are better ignored, but some if they were water wouldn't even slide off a duck's back. So I determined to take on Harry the Hunk or my mind would never be set at ease as long as I worked on this job.

By this time I've been on the job a while and I've gotten to know the crew of mechanics in my shop. They turned out to be a pretty good group after all. Dave struck me as a Hell's Angel type at first glance. Kinda scruffy, his beard half grown out. Yeah, I know that's in style now, but believe me on him it looked scruffy. Skinny as a cotter pin and at least six three. Drives a Harley. He's the first to talk to me. "Don't let 'em get to you," he says. "I know what you're going through. My wife's a sheet metal apprentice."

I'm like, no kidding. We were instant friends.

Well, that broke the ice. The others might have been a little jealous of Dave, or they might have decided I'm no more different from any of them than they are from each other. Two are immigrants, from Ireland and El Salvador. The rest are blacks, whites, and Chicanos.

We circled around each other for a while, testing limits. I had to tell one or two not to call me girl or honey. Had to thank them for their offers of help, but let them know I've got two arms, I can carry things just like taller people. Maybe better, 'cause I'm closer to the ground.

I did almost get into a scrape with the foreman, Fernando, a very proper Catholic gentleman who let me know in so many words he thinks women belong at home and not in a garage earning a man's wage. In his world women don't leave their children to go to work, they don't wear pants, and they don't swear.

Now all my friends know I can cuss a streak as blue as any longshoreman. I let the guys know swearing doesn't bother me at all. So I'm starting to feel real comfortable in the shop, and one day I'm shooting the breeze with Fernando trying to tell him I deserve a good job, I've got three kids to support just like him, when I guess I let a four-letter word drop. Well, he gets this look on his face all kind of furrowed and scrunched. I swear the corners of his mouth drooped more than his mustache. His eyes turned into little black ball bearings under his bushy brows. Then he draws himself up and says, "Dear, I don't see any reason to use that word."

'Course I know this is not true, since I hear the guys say it all the time. What he means is he has a different standard for women and men. Well, you know I'll fight for a lot of things, but my right to swear at work is not first on my list. So I say, "Okay, Fernando, I'll make a deal with you. I'll never swear in front of you again, if from now on you call me Bev instead of dear." He thinks this is an honorable agreement, and we even shake on it, though I suspect he doesn't think women ought to shake either.

Turns out Fernando took me seriously. Called me by my name from then on. I've kept my part too, ever since, and our truce stood me in good stead in my ongoing battle with Harry the Hunk. Fernando could see what was going on. So, after that, when Harry would come through the shop, before he could even get his big mouth open, Fernando would yell at him, "Heeeey sweeetheart."

This should have been enough to make any grown man blush, but Harry just took it in stride. He'd smile sheepishly and go about his business. But he wouldn't stop calling me sweetheart.

Then one day I hear Harry lay the same trip on Dave. "Hey, hippie," he says, "when are you gonna get a haircut?" Harry's smiling the whole time, but I can tell Dave doesn't think it's funny. Dave just keeps his mouth shut and concentrates on his brake job.

Harry keeps smiling at me, too, and I start to figure out the only way he knows how to be friendly is harassing people. But I decide I don't care, I never liked being called names and I'm not gonna get used to it. If he wants to make friends he's got to at least learn my name.

One day I put it to him. "Harry," I say, "why do you keep calling me sweetheart when you know I hate it?"

"You hate it?" he says. "But I call my wife sweetheart and she loves it."

"Harry, I'm not your wife, I'm your coworker, Bev. I'm not your sweetheart." Now I'm thinking this guy is thick. He really doesn't get it. This is gonna be harder than I thought.

A while later he brings in his truck for emergency work and I'm the only mechanic available. "Come on," he says, "hop to it, sweetheart. I gotta get this baby back on the road."

"Harry," I say, "either you never learned the mechanics' law or you forgot it."

"Mechanics' law, what's that?" he says.

"Very basic," I say. "The law says you treat your mechanic right, you got a smooth running truck. Treat your mechanic bad and your truck never gets out of the shop. Harry, if you don't stop calling me sweetheart, you could be a permanent pedestrian."

"Okay, okay," he says, "if it means that much to you. I really need my truck...Bev."

I could see his mouth had great difficulty forming the word, but it was a start. After that, he seemed to try harder. He'd bolt into the shop in his usual back slapping, shoulder punching way and yell, "Hey, Swee...Bev." This was a great improvement, and I told myself I'd made progress, but Harry seemed to be having a hard time making the transition. I couldn't tell whether his harassment had taken a new form or his mind just wasn't making the connection.

Now that we're "friends" Harry thinks he can take new liberties. One day he lopes over, yells, "Hey Swee...Bev," and wraps his arms around me in a bear hug. I duck, but not soon enough, and he gets me in a headlock.

I growl at him, "Harry, what are you doing?"

He looks hurt. "Just saying hello."

So after that whenever he sees me he holds his arms outstretched as if to hug me and gets this sad teddy bear lost puppy look on his face. God, I think, I've created a monster.

"Jeez, Harry, go hug an I-beam."

Harry finally learns to say my name without having to stop and think every time. Natural as can be, he comes in and says, "Hey, Bev, how ya doin'?" We chitchat about our kids, I ask him how his wife puts up with him. He tells me she's really a liberated woman. I start to actually like the guy, but as soon as I let him know that, he thinks all the rules are off. He thinks he can call me whatever he wants and I'll go along with the program.

I run into him as I'm hurrying across the yard on my way back from lunch break. "Hey, sweetheart," he grins, arms outstretched as he walks toward me. I can see if I keep walking I'll head right into his grasp, so I have to stop and move sideways like a crab to avoid him.

When this happens, I frown, cross my arms, look him straight in the eye and say something like, "Harry, go drive your truck off a cliff." I'm trying to let him know I'm not playing, but to him this is the game.

One day he walks into the shop with a woman. I should say amazon. This woman's gotta be six feet tall. Built like a linebacker. Her skin is the color of Colombian coffee. Her black hair is knotted up under a red kerchief and she's dressed in work clothes and boots, so she's got to be working here. Another woman in the yard! I'm thinking, who is she, what does she do, when Harry brings her right over to introduce me.

"Sweetheart," he booms, "I want you to meet my new partner, Pam."
He's grinning so wide, his teeth take up half his face.

Now people say I'm easygoing. I'm known for my high boiling point.
But I swear when Harry says this I feel like an engine overheating.
Smoke must be coming out of my ears. I have to hold my arms next to
my sides to keep from strangling him, and I start yelling all the words I
promised Fernando I wouldn't.

"Aww, come on," he whines, "I was only kidding."

"Harry," I hiss, "don't call me sweetheart. It's not funny, it was never
funny, and it's never gonna be funny."

When he turns around and walks out of the shop I hope I never see the
jerk again. I also hope Pam doesn't think I'm a total nut case. I do want
to talk to her. But a little while later Harry slinks back in, alone this time,
and stands beyond punching distance from me, head hanging, and says
in a low voice, "Bev, I'm really sorry. You know I didn't mean to make
you mad. I was just showing off to my new partner. I promise, I'll never
do it again."

"Right," I say, and jerk my socket wrench so hard I take a slice of skin
off my thumb knuckle when it hits the block.

By this time I don't trust Harry the Hunk for a minute, and I tell myself
I'm never gonna get set up again. So I just try to avoid him and be real
busy whenever he comes by. He still acts friendly and says hi and I try to
be civil. He always calls me Bev, still yelling as loud as ever. And
because I'm not a person who can hold a grudge, I loosen up and let my
defenses down some. Pretty soon we're back to our old routine. But he's
never called me sweetheart since.

One day he stops by and gives me a hand with a generator I'm trying
to move. "Thanks," I say. "I don't care what they say about you. You're
okay."

"Hey, Bev," he grins, "all that work paid off. I turned out okay, huh."

"Yeah, Harry," I say, "and it only took me five years."

Photo by Sandy Thacker

Definitions
Sue Doro

CHEATER BAR — "Macho" term for long pipe
                              used to slide over wrench handles
                              to obtain greater leverage.

                              She
                              didn't like
                              the name.

                              Reclaimed it:

PIPE — An extension of power, effective,
                              persistent, strong

                              Like a woman
                              in a nontraditional
                              job.

Facts
Sue Doro

Dedicated to my sister Tradeswomen

somewhere between days when we can't find anything good to say
about being a woman in a nontraditional job and
the times when we feel like Amazons is
the fact of getting up to go to work each day
every day at five in the morning winter dark Wisconsin
snow covering the goddamn car
dig the stupid thing out so you can go to work
where you know there'll be ice on the steel axles and wheels
you're supposed to machine and the ice will fly off in chunks
and hit your hard hat and make you glad you have it on for once
not like in the summer when it's so hot the micrometer readings
aren't accurate and you just want to go to the beach and
lie all day like a fig or a tobacco leaf or a peach
and the fact is it's work to go to work and
harder when you get there and harder yet
when you're the only woman and you're forced to choose
what clothes to even put on in the morning
or afternoon or night depending on what shift you're on
and what pants to wear that don't show this or that and
what shirt to cover your tits and that's the way it is
if you want to make some money to support yourself and your family
legally in this society and you're a woman and you're working
in a factory or a dock or a construction site and
the other people that work there are all men
and you start to feel your power your muscles in your arms
in your legs and it feels good and you don't take shit from anyone
and the nice guys are nice
the shitty guys are shitty
the ones in between are nice some days and shitty other days

and then there's some that are never nice
who are awful who want you gone or dead but for sure not there
but the money is good is necessary and you learn to keep the boss away
and the shitty guys away and the nice guys even help
once in a while and you make friends more than enemies
and you teach every day every day and you learn
how to do your job better than all of them
because you have to just to stay equal whatever that means
and you get very very very tired
and that's a fact

Photo by Sandy Thacker

The Cultural Worker

Sue Doro

The poem waited for her outside the wheel shop door. Waited, as if it were one of the leaning train wheels stacked against each other, like round brown five hundred pound dominoes. Train wheels waiting to be hauled inside the factory, machined to order, then mounted on shiny steel axles and rolled out the door into the Menomonee Valley train yard.

So too, the poem waited. It had been waiting for her to finish work since 3:30 that afternoon. Now it was midnight. Soon she would step out of second shift into the dark of the going home night.

Hours ago in the early evening, the summer sun hung low and rosy over old freight cars in the yard. The poem had gone to the window nearest the machine the woman was operating that night. The poem thought that the sunset would surely get her attention. But not tonight. She was measuring a train axle with a micrometer, straining on her tiptoes to reach around its diameter. The poem could see she was too busy to be thinking poem words, so it did what it knew how to do.

It waited. Measuring minutes against the sun's shadows on the dirty cream-colored brick wall. It waited, as five o'clock break time came. It waited and watched through a different window as the woman ate half of her sandwich sitting at the lunch table by the men's locker room, sharing a newspaper and talking with some of the guys. She was the only woman in the shop. There used to be two others but they got laid off. Now she was the only one of her kind left, and sometimes she was lonely. But tonight the poem saw that she was having a good time, joking with her "buddies."

It was an hour and a half later when the poem looked in again. The woman was standing with the micrometer in her hand, listening to a short elderly man with grey-brown whiskers. He wore a work-worn green hard hat, low over his eyes. His hands glistened with dark brown dirty train bearing grease. In one, he held a red-handled putty scraper. In the other, by their cuffs, a pair of oily rubber gloves. The ring finger was missing on that hand. A cigarette bobbed up and down from his mouth as he talked, its ashes dusting the man's brown shirt every so often. The poem could catch only a few of the man's words—"wife...divorce... still love her...the kids don't..." The woman was intent on listening to the man. The poem went back to wait at the door until dinner break.

In summer it was still light at eight in the evening, and the poem knew that the woman would come outside to sit on the long bench against the building. Most of the men would go out for dinner to the tavern up the hill, so she would usually be alone. Sometimes she would take a walk by the railroad tracks, heading under the freeway. There was a river to watch and listen to, and wild flowers to pick. In the early spring, there were little green onions and asparagus hidden in the tall grasses. Sometimes she would read or write in her journal. But tonight she had no pad of paper, no pencil or pen. She was sitting on the bench, but she was leaning forward a bit, holding a book. A union agreement. And she was not alone. She and some other workers were talking words like "lost jobs...bankruptcy...layoffs beginning in July...the company can't...illegal...they'll try...four guys fired..." The poem saw it was useless to try to get into her head. Then the factory whistle blew and a foreman appeared in the doorway, motioning the woman and the men back to work.

The poem stayed outside.

At ten o'clock the poem went to look in the window by the woman again. She was staring out into the blackness of the night, but she didn't notice the poem. Her eyes were taking in the silhouettes of the axles and wheels and oil drums. Watching black birds fly in front of the huge pink street lights on tall poles that illuminated the train yard. Her face was feeling a good west wind blowing in. She wasn't thinking poem thoughts. She was thinking of going home and wishing the night would hurry so she could get there. "A few more axles," is what she was thinking, as she turned away from the warm starry night. A night smelling of Menomonee Valley city wilderness, and not the stockyards, thanks to the west wind. Away from the window she turned. Away from the poem looking in her window, and back to her job.

33

And finally it was midnight. The moon was high over the factory roof. The yard was a watercolored wash of moonlight and pink from the lights in the valley. The moon was a white ball with a golden ring. The poem waited with the moon, holding its breath. The pink lights shone down over the top of the building, casting shadows on the path next to the tracks.

The woman would be the first ready to leave. Usually she waited for the guys by the little grey door at the far end of the shop. But tonight she told them she was in a hurry. She stepped alone into the night as the midnight whistle blew. She was short, but her shadow was ten feet tall. She carried a paper sack of dirty work clothes in her arms. The poem was with her like her shadow, walking quickly. The farther from the building, the taller her shadow grew, from the pink lights and the moon on her shoulders. Little rocks and pebbles at her feet crunched under her shoes. Each pebble had its own shadow, like pink moon rocks under her feet. She smiled to herself, enjoying the moment.

A cat meowed, and scampered under a parked freight car. Night birds called. Now her shadow split in two, growing taller, taller, taller. Catching pink lights on more poles in the train yard. She stepped carefully across one, two, three sets of tracks. Past stacks of unmachined axles and rows of wheels. Past lines of mounted wheels and axles waiting to be shipped out. A lone black bird cawed at her from a telephone wire. Something stirring in her brain. Some disjointed words seemed to come together. She laughed aloud, and the crow cawed again, leaving its perch to fly over her head into the blackness beyond the realm of pink lights. Then suddenly the woman threw her head back and yelled up into the pink and black sky. "Hey . . .I'm a midnight rider. A cat's eye glider. I'm a second shift lady goin' home!"

She laughed again. And surprised and delighted, the poem jumped inside her like a fetus kicking in the ninth month. She hurried along, faster now, almost running the last few yards past the shanty.

She was at her car in the parking lot now. She unlocked its door, opened it, and flung her sack of dirty clothes in the back seat. Getting in, she started the car up and aimed it out of the lot, waving to the other workers who were now crossing the tracks behind her. Finally she would have time for herself. She felt the uneasy urgency she'd had all night go from her in a deep earth moving sigh as she drove past the guard shanty and turned up the road to the ramp leading from the valley.

And a poem was born, comfortable as a well fitting work shoe and satisfying as the end of a work day. The poem. The woman. The machinist. All became one. And she sang to the hum of her car:

> *I'm a midnight rider*
> *A cat's eye glider*
> *I'm a second shift woman goin' home*
>
> *I'm a moon rock walker*
> *A night bird stalker*
> *I'm a short tall shadow headin' home*
>
> *I'm a cool old river*
> *A seasoned survivor*
> *I'm a factory workin' poet goin' home.*

On Sunday

Elaine Starkman

I washed the toilet
took a shower
trimmed my hair
and wore a yellow sundress
to lunch with friends
who paint as much as
I write
only *they* don't think
themselves painters

At Mother Nature's
I ordered coffee
instead of herbal tea
and didn't think about
writing
for sixty minutes

I was nearly normal
for one whole day

If Only

Jane Ellen Ibur

I know I can write if I can just get my study really together, really functional. When I finish that wall with the new, longer boards, and I space those boards out rather than having the books two deep on the shelves, I know I'll be ready. I just need to file those copies of other stories, poems, notes, ideas. I know that when I get them in the file cabinet, I'll be that much closer to being ready. If I just clear my desk, organize the top so there's room to write, put some new ballpoints in my favorite pens, wipe the dust, start a new notebook, I'll be ready. Right after I scrape the paint from the windowpanes behind my desk.

If I just finish that touch-up painting on the hallway leading to my study, all will be in readiness. If I patch that crack in the bedroom, get more water pressure to the shower, clean the toilet, I'll have time to write. I just have to wash the stairs to the secret hallway once more and I think I'll finally have that plaster dust under control. And then I can paint those walls and lay some carpeting. If I finish building that spaceship in the secret hallway, I know I'll be inspired to write. If I just had two comfortable couches in the den.

If I could be assured that my fourteen-year-old cat is thin because it's so hot and not because she's dying, if I had a dining room set, I'd be ready to write. If I caulked that stairway leading to the basement, if I swept the basement, if I moved the barbecue pit back to the garage, if I hung those tools in the garage, and put up a new back fence, then I could really write.

If my vegetable garden and flowers survive better next year, I know I'll blossom as a writer. If I could just get to the grocery store. If I could just stop worrying about this sudden hair loss I'm having, I know I could concentrate, focus, and write. If I just had clean hair.

If I could compose at the typewriter instead of having to write in longhand first, if I had a computer, if my teeth were cleaned, if my bowels were regular, I know I could go write.

If I were a better cook I'd be a better writer. Organization in the kitchen begets organization in the study. If I had more sex I'd be mellow enough. If my ankle would heal, if only I could jog again, then I'd be in good shape to write. If I lost ten pounds I'd be confident enough.

If I were just a little happier, I know I could write. If I were just a little taller, that would do it for sure. If I could just have a little equilibrium, a little hope, a little serenity. If I could just have one year of total harmony, I know I'd be at peace enough to write. If I could just get over my past, I'd be able to write about it. If I just felt secure, if I knew my mother really loved me, if I were pretty, I know I could write. If I could just finish therapy, I know I'd be ready.

If I can just get through this one lifetime, I know I'll be ready and able to write.

Star

Jacklyn Potter

You said sing, Daddy,
and I sang with melodies
lilting through my baby
shoelaces; down into my eyes
fell the starlight of yours.
And my red heart filled
your repertoire.

Let's hear some songs,
you said, for Red Cross
war veterans and heroes and Chambers
of Commerce. My braids
glistened and my hands tossed
kisses to hundreds of hands
clattering praise.

You said sing, Daddy,
and school days ended early
with a microphone
in my hand. My smile
and the rose in my hair
were on the air.

Perfect and best
I sang and heard your banjo
ring.

You said sing.
Read through these watermarks.
Your starlight falls from these eyes.
Can you hear this scratching on the page?

Daddy, I am singing.

Photo by Clytia Fuller

Preamble
Elizabeth Gilliland

Before I can paint I must think
a thousand thoughts, redo
my philosophy, change fans
in my studio and read the ten
books I have underway; before
I can paint I must relive
what is left of childhood scripts,
dip into springs of what flows

what is my muse whose wings
hover beside me, who stuffs
my pillow at night with a poem;
before I can paint I must buy
all the supplies for a long space
free of trips to the art store.
The eye as portal of love
is not my muse though it can

lift me above all existence,
the years of journey is not
my muse though after you tell
your story, in the night hot tears
spill that on waking leave me
freed for a spell and it is in
this space, however evanescent,
that I begin to make my art.

Handmade Book

Elizabeth Gilliland

If colors of day are shaped by sun
and marble can store memory of earth,
paper can find the present

lift it from the vat of beaten stuff
full of flaws and accidents —
traces of flax guided

into place by the hand
that throws off the mold.
Laid lines trap energies from

eye to wrist as the sheet moves
together. We work at a craft
imprinting our own rhythms

translating gesture into ritual.
Twenty centuries haven't changed
tool and material finding

each other. Fibers merge and link
never losing what they are.
Deckle pages close

and are tied with straw.

Teaching

Katharyn Machan Aal

I have begun to tell the students
my politics: always dangerous
in box-shouldered academe, walls
where whispers strike thin cracks,
widen, echo, suck. I speak
of women's bodies, choice, language
that keeps men men but makes of women
girls, chicks, cunts, slits, pieces
of a twisted dream of domination.
The eighteen year olds in their warm socks stare
all pink and green, small alligators
dancing on their shirts. One mutters
"women's lib," daring just that much
against the red ink my pen wields.
They will write home to mothers and fathers—
or, most likely, call collect—and tell
of the teacher who wears her hair long,
who says strange things that have nothing to do
with them, their needs, their nights, their money,
the jobs they will hold in four years.

Term Paper

Mary Pierce Brosmer

Today
I graded
a term paper:
"The Recovery
of Anorexics."

The girl
had written:
"I decided on
this topic because
right now
my sister
is dieing
of
starvation."

I corrected
the spelling —
dieing —
because
I could not
correct
the
dying.

I wept
for
them both,
us all,

starving.

Photo by Lori Burkhalter-Lackey

Sprezzatura
Maxine Combs

Instead of mowing the lawn and clipping the pyracantha hedge this late August Saturday, my husband Eli sits at the kitchen table and talks about his grandfather.

"The old man moved to Miami Beach in 1912 from a Polish town that no longer exists. He took a room on Flagler Avenue and began looking for work, but his Polish name counted against him. Prospective employers shook their heads: too long, too unpronounceable, too harsh, too foreign."

Eli tells this story to nineteen-year-old Larry, our son, who has stopped by on his way to work. Larry, wearing a black T-shirt and a silver ring on every finger, is making a Spanish omelet and only half listening. He cracks four eggs into a bowl, adds grated cheese, onions, red and green peppers, salt.

Eli becomes animated. He waves a muscular arm and puts on his glasses, as if the lenses will magnify his memory. "The old man wanted to get ahead," Eli says, "so he decided to change his name. He stared out the window and found inspiration. He became Mr. Flagler."

Larry foams butter in a pan, pours in his eggs.

Eli sips from his blue-rimmed coffee mug. "You know what happened then?" he asks.

Larry, who has heard this story dozens of times, shakes his head, no.

"He went into real estate, did very well. And sixty years later everyone assumed Flagler Avenue had been named after him."

"Try some of this omelet," Larry says.

"Don't mind if I do," Eli says.

At my new job I sit at my desk imagining I'm delivering a lecture on *sprezzatura*. *Sprezzatura* is a sixteenth century word that describes art that doesn't seem like art. Art that appears easygoing, effortless, effervescent. The term, I believe, had to do with Sidney or Castiglione.

I will never deliver my imaginary lecture. I was not hired to teach Renaissance Literature. I was hired—a week ago—to teach four sections of Freshman Composition. I was hired to accommodate an overflow of students caused by an unexpected six percent increase in enrollment.

On my desk sits a complimentary copy of *Current Issues and Enduring Questions* which juxtaposes essays by Gloria Steinem ("I get the feeling that most women are speaking Urdu and most men are speaking Pali") and Plato ("People do not learn things; they remember them").

This is not the text the department uses, merely one they once considered. How it landed on my desk I cannot say.

This is the second week of classes, but I have not entered a classroom. The Administration is still vetting my credentials. They want to check my resume, my transcripts, my references. They want to ascertain that Rose Flagler is who she says she is. I'm curious as to whether they will succeed. If it turns out I am not who I say I am, I wonder...who will I turn out to be?

My friend's daughter Valerie has become interested in that Arabic document, attributed to Hermes Trismegistus, known as *The Emerald Table*:

> That which is above is like to that which is below, and that
> which is below is like that which is above.

This doctrine, which became the basis for medieval alchemy, sought to "summarize the principles of change in Nature."

Valerie's mother is worried. She telephoned to tell me that in the last month Valerie has bought two decks of tarot cards and a stack of books on the occult.

Valerie and Larry are exactly the same age. Sylvia Watson—Valerie's mother—was my roommate in the hospital when we were both having our babies. The kids played together when they were small, but in later years drifted apart.

Larry works as a chef. His ambition is either to operate a catering business or to play drums in a band that crisscrosses the country.

Valerie says she wants to be a witch.

Once Eli flew Yellow Perils for the U.S. Navy, but these days he avoids parking under trees (branches might fall), sleeping in drafts (they cause colds), or reading newspapers in light-colored pants (the newsprint rubs off). When Larry was younger, Eli read him accounts of disasters from the newspapers. "A teenager suffered serious injury when he stuck his feet out the back window of the family car, and the car was sideswiped by a city bus. The seventeen year old is expected to lose one foot."

Larry never paid attention. Throughout his childhood, he tested the limits of every teacher and was asked to leave four different schools. He rides his bike through red lights at rush hour, makes a dinner out of banana cake and beer, plays his drums until four a.m. I call him up at the group house where he lives now with advice on how to clean up his act. His inevitable response is, "Hey, someone else here wants to use the phone. Can I call you back later?"

Eli also has a story about his ex-wife's grandfather. This time he's telling the story to Sylvia and Richard, Valerie's parents.

"This guy had asthma as a kid, and he'd heard the Denver climate was just what he needed. So he went to check it out. This was in—I don't know the exact year—early in the century. Anyway, he got off the train and looked around for a cab. He couldn't find one, so he seized his bags and boxes and staggered off towards the nearest rooming house. The next day he paid the first installment on an automobile, learned to drive it, returned to the station, and launched himself into the taxi business. He ended up owning the biggest fleet of cabs in Denver."

"Wow," Sylvia says. "Bought a car and learned to drive it the same day."

"Those guys didn't mess around," Richard says.

Valerie, who has been reading in a corner, closes her book and stands up.

She is a tall girl, her hair jaggedly cut and dyed jet-black, her eyes so heavily made up they look hooded.

"My friend Wendy's mother only makes $5.35 an hour after working for seven years at K-Mart," she says.

"She needs another job," Sylvia says.

Sylvia doesn't work.

The conversation shifts to Valerie's new job in a soap store that sells items like red jasmine cologne or gardenia bath gel. She has started at $4.50 an hour.

She offers me marigold hand cream from a sample tube.

"Ummm." I rub some in.

"Marigolds mean someone wants to know more about you," she says.

"That's the University Administration rechecking my credentials," I say.

"Poor Rosie," Eli says.

"So much red tape," Sylvia says.

"Mimosa means second thoughts," Valerie reads from a pamphlet.

"What's the flower that means you're contemplating wandering on and on in a vast forest without thought of return?" I feel myself getting into the flower-as-symbol mode.

"I'll have to look that one up," Valerie says.

Both Larry and Eli prefer bottled to tap water. Last spring Eli read a newspaper account about a neighborhood where lead was found in the drinking water of several houses. He sent a sample of our water to be tested and, although it showed a negligible lead content, he began carting home gallons of Polar water from the supermarket.

Larry uses this water for ice cubes.

I watch him fill four ice trays.

"No sense drinking pure water with impure ice cubes," he says, sliding the brimming trays into the freezer compartment.

"Are you really worrying about impure ice cubes?" I ask.

Larry raises an eyebrow. "What if I get the hiccoughs and have to swallow ice?"

"Right," I say. I'm drinking a cup of tea — brewed from tap water — and scanning the morning paper. It's a Saturday.

Larry sits down, riffles papers until he finds the comics, reads for a minute, looks up and asks, "What do you worry about?"

"The disguises of the self," I say without thinking.

"Whoa!" Larry says. "The disguises of the self! What about the Greenhouse Effect? Nuclear War? Forest fires in Yellowstone Park? Floods in Bangladesh?"

"I worry about that stuff too."

"I worry about only making seven dollars an hour when there's another guy at the restaurant who makes eight."

"Why does he make more?"

"More experience. He opens the place up. I'd like his job."

"Is he thinking about quitting?"

"People quit all the time."

"They do?" The world Larry's describing doesn't seem familiar.

"Sure," he says. He pours a glassful of bottled water and we both watch the bubbles stream to the top. "People quit all the time," he repeats. "There's a girl in my house who's had six jobs in three weeks."

"Easy come, easy go," I say. The water in the glass is still now.

Larry gulps it down.

"What do you mean about disguises of the self?" he asks then.

"Oh, as one self, characters in books seem realer than life. As another I'm a leaf from a tree, an expression of nature. As another, I'm an outsider, restricted to the observations and memories of my ego, not really connected to anything or anybody."

"Yeah," Larry says. "I know what you mean. Some days I'd like to machine gun everyone I know and go live in the Arizona desert. And some days I think I'm falling in love with my boss. You just can't tell."

On Monday of the third week of the semester, I receive word that I've been cleared and that I should report to my classes.

On Tuesday I'm informed that one of my composition sections is to be replaced by a Survey of American Literature, and that the students have started *The Scarlet Letter.*

I dig out my copy and begin to reread the story of Hester Prynne.

On Friday I'm told my schedule has changed again and I will lose another composition section and pick up a class in Advanced Essay Writing.

I knock on the chairman's door.

"Do you think my schedule is set now?" I ask.

The chairman flashes a disarming smile. "Never can tell around here," she says.

"I've noticed that," I say.

"I think you're set," she says. "There's not much more we can do to you."

I trot over to the campus bookstore where I find that the anthology ordered for the American Lit class will not be available for eight weeks, and that another section has taken all the books ordered for my Advanced Essay class.

I go home and climb in bed for a nap.

Later, Eli takes me out to dinner where, over whiskey sours and fried shrimp, I fill him in.

"I like the new classes," I say. "But not one of the books is available."

"That's tough," Eli says. "What are you going to do?"

"I've considered suicide in the main aisle of the bookstore."

Eli shakes his head. "Too messy."

"We could spend all semester on *The Scarlet Letter*."

"I always liked Hawthorne," Eli says.

"Me too."

"Guess you'll just have to wing it."

"Umm," I say.

Eli's ex-wife has married four times since their divorce. When they were together she changed her job every few months. She worked in a framing store for six weeks, then quit because her boss was grouchy. She found a new job in a bookstore where they wanted her to work the cash register, but she didn't like numbers. Then she found a job in telemarketing, but everyone in the office smoked.

"A mover-on," Eli says about her.

It's another Saturday afternoon. The lawn still needs mowing, but I don't mention it. Instead, I ask, "Were you devastated at the breakup?"

Eli stacks newspapers as if he were building a stone wall.

"We both had the seven-year itch," he says. "A hundred years ago."

Not quite a hundred years ago. They were married from 1960 to 1967.

Eli and I got together in 1968.

Still, I know what he means; I'm also the veteran of an early unsuccessful marriage.

"I'm not planning to get married at all," says Larry who's stopped by on his way to the restaurant. He's dressed in jeans and a T-shirt that says Feed the Homeless.

"Someday you may change your mind," I say.

"And fight the way you guys used to? No way." Larry removes a newspaper from the pile Eli has stacked, fishes a stubby pencil from a pocket, and begins to scratch at the crossword puzzle.

"Us fight?" Eli asks, amazed.

"Oh my god," Larry says. "Don't funny me."

"Well, you seem to have survived," I say.

"Naturally hardy, I guess."

"Right," I say.

The phone rings and Eli answers it in the den.

Larry stares at the newspaper. "What's Jason's vessel?" he asks. "Four letters."

"A-R-G-0," I say.

He fills in squares.

"I might marry Melissa," Larry says then. "She's one of the girls in my house. We've discussed it. She said if she ever married anyone, it would be me."

"Melissa's got good taste," I say.

"Then there's my boss. I'm in love with her, but she's too old. She's thirty-three."

"You've got plenty of time."

"My last girlfriend was twenty-six. I guess I'm attracted to older women."

"Sounds like it."

"They make me grow up faster."

"You're doing all right," I say.

"I am?" Larry looks pleased. "But not on this puzzle. I never finish them. Melissa's pretty good. She sits down and whips right through them." He shoves the paper across the table, stands up. "You finish it," he says. "I'm off to work."

"See you later," he shouts into the den, then slams out the front door.

A minute later Eli emerges.

"Someone taking a survey," he says about the phone call. Then he rushes to the front door.

"Hey, Larry," he shouts. "Come back here. I want to give you a Radon Testing Kit. Thirty percent of houses have radon leakage."

"I'll get it another time," Larry shouts back from halfway down the block. "Hang onto it for me, will you?"

It's almost the end of September. The weather is golden and warm, and yesterday Eli and I walked along the canal admiring the asters and jewelweed.

My classes have settled down. I xeroxed 300 pages from *The Norton Anthology* and distributed them to the American Lit class. For Advanced Essay I asked the students to write an essay and we've been discussing the results.

I mention my xeroxing to Sylvia in a late night telephone conversation.

"Isn't that illegal?" she asks.

"I'd have the students buy the books," I say, "if they were available."

"Hmmm," Sylvia says.

"How's Valerie?" I ask, hoping to deflect Sylvia's attention.

"She's reading *The Egyptian Book of the Dead*. She stayed out till six a.m. the other night. When we sat down to play bridge on Saturday, we discovered she'd taken the queen of hearts out of every deck of cards in the house. We ended up playing Scrabble."

I sympathize.

"It's not easy having a grown-up child living at home," Sylvia says.

"At least she's working," I say.

"Cross fingers."

After we hang up, I sit and stare out the window.

A soft rain has started to fall.

Eli's already in bed.

My head is crammed with fleeting images: the queen of hearts, Hester

Prynne, Wendy's mother whose salary is $5.35 an hour.

All those impractical stubborn women.

I imagine them, lost and anxious, awkward and ecstatic, as they hurry home after work or some important errand, wrapped in raincoats at least seven years old, yet sporting an odd glittering brooch or earrings glowing with real pearls.

A band of adventurers about to set sail passes by in the opposite direction. Grandfathers and young boys, their heads full of schemes, keep refusing to capitulate to forces that would shape them like wire fences around city trees. They embark on a secret seven year journey, forgetting to say good-bye, forgetting the rain, forgetting the name of the place they're sailing towards. They notice the open purple sky, the rain-ravelled waves, the sea sounds mingling with the ship sounds. They sail on. On and on.

I pad into the kitchen, pour bourbon into a glass, fill it with ice and bottled water. The bubbles swirl to the surface, but before I resume my seat by the window they have all evaporated into nothingness.

Photo by Marianne Gontarz

Interview

Susanna Rich

First, you are outnumbered: three to ten of them —
one of you. Each leans on your vita
as if it were a placemat.
You wear an interview suit: starched labels
fidget from your coccyx to your knotted neck.

They sit you in the preheated depressions
of another candidate's nervousness
and swirl your mind into an alphabet soup of names
you could never remember, bubbles of eyes,
smiles of string beans. Their manicured fingers fist
around pencils, twist studded rings. Your tongue
swells into a ripe apple, too large to form
the right words, too slick for you to bite in time.

Then one pinches your collar, to see if you're
100% or merely synthetic. Another thrusts
a business card under your arm, to litmus
whether you eat poly or unsaturated. That
something thin worming into your right ear,
coming out the left, is mental floss.
Two of them saw it back and forth
slicing through the length of you.

They open you like a refrigerator to see
if the light goes on. One inspects
your drawers for uneaten spinach and decades
of unfinished glasses of milk.
He calibrates your tomatoes while another
toasts the quality of your cold cuts and buns.
A third times cracked egg oozing
behind your ears. Two of them
unscrew your shelves with dimes and shake you
like a pinball machine—to see if they can score.
Meanwhile you must keep cool, preshrunk,
sucking on the apple of your tongue.

Soon you will be trussed with lines
of policy, a chorus of benefits. Buttered up—
the better to slide you through the mail
slot—you leave. They roll your vita
into toothpicks and joints, and wonder if
"Fifteen thou is too little, thirty too much"—
like a commercial wondering how many prunes
to take for regularity.

You will wonder in your bed if you were appetizing,
if you satisfied the silk shirts, the Acapulco
tans, the thick wads of bills burning
in their seats. You will rise hungry,
and illuminated by the light
of your empty refrigerator—
eat your heart out.

Search Committee
Barbara Unger

I refuse to be just another overqualified adjunct professor. This time I've targeted my resume, which is why I have been called to interview while thousands far more gifted than I have been sent form rejections. My resume points to rhetoric and my PC. I have focused it on my recent experience in desktop publishing. Both my creative writing M.F.A. and my background in womens' studies have been excised. *Fleurs du mal*. I wear my pencil-stripe suit with big power shoulders.

The elevators at Municipal go up and down like fever thermometers. My car fills with a gaggle of urban students. It shoots up fifteen floors before I can distinguish one Caribbean accent from another. The halls are orange; the work stations, beige. All one can say of the atmosphere is that it's a tad less than donnish. A secretary in a plaid skirt greets me at the English Department door.

"Hello," she says. "Are you the eleven o'clock candidate?" I nod. She shows me to a chair beside her desk and returns to her green computer screen. I take out Professor Darlene Kalen's letter. "Our major consideration for the position of Instructor of Freshman Composition is a knowledge of publishing and an academic background in pedagogy and rhetoric." At least that much is clear. Since the committee room door is locked, I assume that the Search Committee is running late.

Above the secretary's desk is a picture of a growling panther. "Attack Secretary," the caption reads. Her B.A. is framed on the wall. Against the opposite wall is a John Donne poster: *No man is an island* · · · · I remind myself of this, tapping one foot nervously on the orange carpet. The lame mailcart boy appears at the door.

"Good morning, Juan," says the secretary, as he shoves mail into the faculty boxes. His handicap doesn't halt his determination. As he hobbles past, he smiles. I take heart.

"They're running late," explains the secretary with a smile. I nod and remove a pad from my attaché case. From then until nearly noon, as the secretary taps at the computer, I wriggle in my chair, writing on the pad. Actually I am crafting an erotic encounter between my blonde heroine, Samantha Shaw, and the dark-haired hero, Brad or will he be a Shane? Leicester Publishers, in its romance novel guidelines, suggests that the heroine be a virgin. This is the very same Leicester Publishers that appears on my resume under "Knowledge of Editing and Publishing."

From time to time, I feel pointillist pricks in my duodenum, a Seurat painting, and glance for the hundredth time at my curriculum vitae. The idea of a real job with tenure, medical insurance, and a pension plan makes me anxious. I hope I won't have to answer too many hostile questions the way I did at my last interview.

In my attaché case, I have an unanswered letter from my mother. It's hard to explain to her how my background in Virginia Woolf and the poems I published in obscure quarterlies are a liability when it comes to getting a garden-variety, entry-level college teaching position. I cannot fault her for this. She says writing romance books under a pseudonym doesn't put me in the right circles. She has a point here as well. Finally my name is called.

I observe the ten o'clock candidate shaking hands with Darlene at the door and secure everything in the attaché. Then I stride into the committee room and take my seat. The Search Committee is still thumbing through its folders trying to figure out who the hell I am. The secretary comes to the door, the precise clicking of her heels bringing the committee to attention. She plops down five still-warm xeroxes of my resume. My hands start to sweat trying to think of something to say. My brain goes blank. Instead I study my inquisitors.

One reminds me of everyone's favorite English prof, all tweedy, bearded, with pipe. The second is an elf with protruding teeth. The third is a middle-aged hausfrau-professor, looking much mortgaged and married. And then Darlene, in her royal blue power shoulders. And him!

Hypnotized, I remember everything about him except his name. We had gone to a swank midtown hotel. His wedding ring was plain and dull. We'd wrestled out of our clothes and made love on the peach hotel bedspread, avoiding the hotel logo embroidered into the quilting. We'd showered in the peach tub and dried each other's glistening bodies with thick peachy towels. We'd awakened with the taste of too much to drink in our mouths and enjoyed a room-service breakfast. Then we'd split. I'd spoken to him on the phone a few times. I tried to bring the details onto my mental screen. He was a professor of English somewhere. I remember some of the things he'd said about his wife. Didn't all their wives misunderstand them? Some friends had introduced us at this East Village cafe where he'd been slumming and where I had just read my poetry at the open mike. It was five, six years ago. And now he remembers me with a hurt, puzzled expression.

"Did you have any trouble getting here?" asked the chairperson whom I persist in calling Darlene. She shoots me a good-girl grin and I tell her no, describing my means of transportation, subway and taxi. I sense I've made a friend in Darlene. The committee plunges directly into my editing and publishing experience, to see if I can handle the monthly department newsletter. I talk about graphics, software, fonts, the good life, while they smile, eager to hear my lies. I manage to get through the interrogation without once glancing at his selfish dissipated face, remembering how he made love badly and without passion or consideration.

Meanwhile, as I play with the latest buzzwords and theories — deconstruction, writing across the curriculum — they brim with intellectual curiosity. I begin to think that I have what they really want. I have read Darlene right. Then, a shiver oscillates through the room as my nemesis enters the interrogation.

"It says here," he begins, in one of those cool, understated voices that could bend steel, "that you won the Ann Walker Fearing Poetry Medal at college."

I choke as I remember how, in a reckless moment, I had not deleted that fact from my resume.

"What do you think of Miss Fearing's poetry?" he inquires, running one hand through his long silvery hair as he shoots me a synthetic smile.

Stay noncommittal, a voice inside warns me, sensing a trap. "A competent poet," I reply. Then at once I remember his name. Dick Warren, a Shakespeare man.

I squirm in my seat as the room topples into disaster with silence all around. A look of urgency invades Dr. Kalen's face. Her good-girl smile dissolves. She glares at Dick Warren with a look that would freeze lava and I realize that I've created a rift in the room just the right size for a Mack truck.

"Dick, you know how I feel about Ann Walker Fearing's work. She was my major professor and more than merely a competent poet, Miss Wanamaker," she says, turning sternly to me and calling me by my name. "I have always felt Ann Fearing was a major but neglected female poet."

Before I can utter a sound, Dick Warren emits a studied baritone groan. "Now let's face it. Even your feminist critics admit that her work resists largeness and depth. Her work simply will not stand up against the work of her contemporaries." His voice, rich in academic disdain, dominates the room. His lids resemble hunched capes as he continues to thrust and parry. "Her work is cramped by a spinster's one-dimensional vision." A second shiver oscillates through the room. All eyes are on me.

Throwing caution to the winds, I plunge in, knowing that I am about to immerse the entire room in controversy. "It's easy to name fifty male poets of her generation whom we regard as significant. Yet it's hard to come up with five women — and not because the quality's not there. To me, Fearing's neglect is the epitome of the plight of the woman writer in masculine culture."

"Are you calling Ann Fearing a prototype feminist?" squeaks the buck-toothed midget.

"Labels, labels," sighs Darlene, dismissing the comment, her mouth firm and unequivocal.

"A second-rate minor poet," says Dick Warren.

The mortgaged hausfrau in her gold chains squirms in her chair.

"One of America's foremost sonneteers," says Darlene.

"Nonsense," says Dick Warren, dismissing the idea as too absurd to debate. "But Miss Wanamaker here seems to agree with your definition. Am I right, Miss Wanamaker?"

All eyes were on me.

"I tend to agree with Professor Kalen." I knew from that moment on, I was doomed with Dick. Don't worry, old Dickie bird, there are still plenty of young bright attractive women who find academic power erotic. I was once one of those easily impressed young women. You'll have others—all is not lost. Beaten, Dick sniffs and Darlene jumps into the void by quizzing me about my knowledge of composition pedagogy. Joylessly, Dick takes me all in. I am a terrible judgment on him. He will not vote for me. Ah, well... Finally it's over; the next candidate in his denims and seersucker jacket is already underneath the "Attack" sign.

"We'll be making our decision by June 30," says Dr. Kalen. I sneak one last look at Dickie. He is packing his papers into his briefcase with his pale precise hands, pretending I'm not there. As I leave, I am met at the door by Darlene Kalen and I study her tense smile. She has a mouth that was set to endure. Insisting on accompanying me to the elevator, she chats about Ann Fearing's eccentricities. As the colloquy continues, I realize she's stalling. Finally, she gropes for my sleeve. "Don't mind my husband. He grills all the applicants like that." My voice began to desert me. "Your husband?"

"Yes. Dick Warren. I keep my maiden name."

"It was a fair interview," I stammer.

"You handled it well."

"Thanks."

"Anyway, I'm the one who makes the final decision." Her eyes sidle over me in a routine exercise of possession. Our eyes meet. She sees nothing. Just then the elevator doors open.

"You'll be hearing from us," she calls into the sliding doors as they swallow me.

As the elevator glides downward, I am oblivious to the chatter around me. A lunatic simper on my face, I struggle to keep from laughing aloud. If I get the job, the three of us—Darlene, Dick, and I—will grow old together, tenured colleagues locked in the internal machinery of English Department intrigue. High farce! I savor the thought of our guilty secret, almost afraid to face the reality that I will probably be called back. Midway to the front doors, he comes up to me.

"I just wanted to be sure it was you."

"It is."

As he realizes my resolve, his mouth goes slack.

"Don't blackball me. I need this job," I mumble.

His eyebrows shoot up in mock surprise. "Why would I want to do a thing like that?"

"Just forget everything. It just happened," I say. Mercifully, a taxi waits at the curb.

Committee Meeting
Lillian Morrison

I'm out of place
like an old rubber boot
sitting up in a tree in winter.
What is it doing there,
stuck, in strange exile?

Does it remember
the plantations, its tropic youth,
its transformation, the fierce
sweat-dripping climate
of jungle births and buddings?

You people who sit,
solemn, inconclusive, dry branches
fearing the axe of disapproval,
what are you to me?
Your language is alien.

Jargon in a stuffy room.
My neighbor puffs on a cigarette.
Outside, it's raining.
I hear the drops hit the window
like a friend signalling.

Women at Thirty

Michele Wolf

A theme after Donald Justice

Women at thirty
Have been long familiar
With the awkward weight of bundles,
And so it is easy to balance
The groceries and the briefcase
While turning the key.

They flip on the news, then collapse
On the couch, whose cushiony comfort
At times seems more loyal
Than any they've known. The local
Newscasters drone. No time to rest: have to
Start up chicken Marengo, dinner for four.

And while sautéing onions,
They consider minutiae: how the burgundy
Skirt needs mending, IBM is 109 a share,
That client at lunch had a crop of potatoes
Adorning his ears and putrescent cologne.
Katie's birthday is Tuesday — buy a card.

The front door opens. A warbling man enters,
Kisses the cook, disappears to change into jeans.
At fifteen, males were alien beings
With weapons between their legs
That made girls pregnant, girls who quietly
Endured responsibility. Fear haunted every

Kiss good night. How mothers fibbed.
These women know the importance of flesh now,
One of the few things they can count on,
Along with the ache of their monthly flow,
The way it comes and then it goes,
Like the tick of a clock.

For Love or Money

Ruthann Robson

Some days, work is just another cup of coffee without Cecile. Since I am now a supervisor, drinking coffee is included in my official state job description. It means I go to the bathroom frequently. And in my bathroom-sized office, I have a quilt of white Styrofoam cups, half-filled with cold coffee, beige from the dried milk, heavy from the solidified sugar. I have a few ceramic mugs on my desk: one with a pattern of ancient women circles that Cecile ordered for me from some craft coven in Wisconsin; one that says "The Best Man for the Job May Be a Woman" that my former coworkers in Miami gave me when I left. In the mugs which seem too heavy to carry all the way to the bathroom, I grow little fungus creatures. Today, I promise myself every morning, I will scrub these gifts, especially the one from Cecile.

The one from my former coworkers, too. I think their chosen slogan was rather inane, but it is the thought that counts. I miss these former coworkers; not them as individuals with problems and habits and boyfriends and second husbands, but them as coworkers. Now, I do not seem to have any coworkers. I call the people I supervise my coworkers, but this is a bureaucratic lie. I evaluate them; they complain about me. The numbers in our paychecks demonstrate our lack of parity. They do not tell me tales of boyfriends and second husbands. I do not tell them amusing anecdotes about Cecile's latest grumpiness, waving my hands like she always does, calling forth the Cecile that inhabits me.

Instead, in my silence, I miss Cecile. I hate work because it takes me away from her. And from Colby, our child. I hate the pull of the long days. I hate the pull of what are termed benefits but which are really necessities, like health insurance for Colby, if not for Cecile. I hate the pull of the state paycheck; the push of it.

The Division of Motor Vehicles is just another state agency in this state capital congealing with state agencies. Before I was pushed into the promotion of M-12 Supervisor, I worked as a M-10 Computer Clerk in the Miami satellite office. Most people think that the town of Tallahassee is a satellite of the city of Miami, but in government many things are opposite of what most people think.

Mostly, I do the same things I did in Miami. I input and retrieve information. This is computer slang for secretarial work. I also answer the phone, trouble-shoot, and handle citizen inquiries. As an M-12, I supervise other people's inputting, retrieving, phone-answering, trouble-shooting, and handling of citizens. Once in a while, I do something vaguely official. The other day I met with three attorneys, two women and a man, who work at the Attorney General's Office. They explain to me that the state is being sued for discrimination, not in hiring, but in issuing drivers' licenses. The state is being accused of demanding more identification for Hispanic-looking applicants than from Anglo-looking ones. The attorneys say they do not think this is true. I say I would not be surprised if it is. The attorneys frown, as if they do not like my answer. The attorneys do not ask each other—"What can you expect from a dyke?"—at least not so that I can hear. The state is not an equal opportunity employer when it comes to the matter of sexual preference, but even the most conservative attorneys like to pretend they are above such petty prejudices.

I am telling Cecile about the attorneys at the Women's Coffeehouse, where no coffee is served because caffeine has been recently added to the list of items that should be avoided as oppressive. Two women leaning against the wall seem to half-listen to our conversation, as Colby escapes from child care and comes to grab Cecile's hand.

"Oh, the boy." The woman with the shorter hair says this, although if I had looked at the other woman first, I would have thought it impossible that any other living creature could have shorter hair than she did.

"Yes," Cecile says, glaring.

"I couldn't help overhearing your conversation," the other woman says. "My name's Elzy. And this is Maura. My lover is an attorney working on the discrimination case."

"With the state?" I ask.

"No. For the plaintiffs." Elzy looks at me pityingly from her perspective of being in a relationship with a politically correct attorney.

"How do you know about the case?" she asks.

"I work at the Division of Motor Vehicles."

"How awful. What could be more boring?" the woman who has been introduced as Maura says. I look over my shoulder for Cecile, but she has returned with Colby to the child care corner where there are more interesting things to do than stand around sipping mineral water and talking about work.

"Don't be rude," Elzy scolds. "She probably loves her work."

"I don't do it for love. I do it for money." I wish Cecile were standing next to me.

"I can think of more interesting things to do for money," Maura winks. "Especially being as cute as you are."

I am silent.

I am not one of those women who can proudly say: I am a former prostitute. I am not one of those women who can fly like a flag the subject of class: I grew up poor. I cannot admit I am damn glad to have a state job.

Even a job where I have to answer the telephone, as if I were "just" a secretary, as if I had not gone to college for a while on a National Merit Scholarship.

I never answer the phone at home, unless I know it is Cecile. At work, I answer and answer the phone. It is rarely Cecile, at least not since Cecile started going back to school. Mostly, it is a disembodied voice wanting to speak to someone's supervisor. I spend hours listening to my own officiousness. I become especially officious when there is a complaint about one of the "girls."

"No girls work here," I say.

"But I was just talking to one," the complainer protests.

"That's impossible," I answer. I pause. I explain: "That would be against state and federal labor laws."

"What?"

"Girls and boys cannot work. Education is compulsory until at least the age of sixteen."

"Let me speak with your supervisor," the voice demands.

"The Governor is out of town today, may I take a message?"

At this point, the caller either disconnects or becomes conciliatory. There is no way to forecast the choice, although I often give myself odds. Fifty-fifty is the best bet.

The odds are usually about ten-to-one that my supervisor, the Honorable Governor of Florida, is out of town, although I can't say that I keep up with his schedule. My more immediate supervisor is a lot like the Governor: they share the same first name, the same gender, the same vaguely criminal squint around the eyes. And they both travel around the state attending meetings with no practical purpose, although the odds are only about two-to-one that my immediate supervisor is out of town on any given work day.

When my immediate supervisor Bob is in town, he never fails to ask me to go out to lunch. I always refuse. Lunch, I think, is dangerous because it is so innocuous. It is supposed to be casual and merely convenient. I am neither a casual nor convenient person. The Governor never invites me to lunch. I suppose he does not dine with queers.

Usually, I sit in my office, drink coffee, and eat the sandwich and fruit Cecile packed for me. I have a pink plastic bag, the color of our bedroom walls, that I use every day. Colby has a Snoopy lunch box that he brings to primary. I have sliced olives on my cream cheese sandwich; Colby does not. I think about Colby when I eat my lunch. I think about Cecile.

Sometimes Bob, not the Governor Bob, but the Division of Motor Vehicles Bob, comes into my office and talks to me while I am eating. Sometimes he talks about his first wife and his second divorce until his words swell my bathroom-sized office. Perhaps because I hate to munch olives in front of people, I find myself talking back. I tell Bob trivialities about Cecile, about Colby. If he finds it odd that my family is unlike his, it does not show beneath his liberal beard.

I like our conversations best when we talk not about our families, but about "the nature of things." We talk the way Cecile and I used to talk before she went back to school. Today, with his knees crossed and cramped on the other side of my desk, Bob is waxing on the nature of romantic love. He is thinking of going back to his first wife.

"Maybe there is that perfect person out there for each of us," he says.

"Maybe," I agree. I think of Cecile.

"But what happens if we do not recognize her when we see her?" he wonders.

"You did," I reassure. "But it is often easy to forget what you remembered."

"Remembered?" he asks.

"Plato's *Symposium*," I answer. We have discussed this all before; even the part where Plato has the characters talking about true love; even the part where we were all really two people but got tragically separated and spend our lives looking for our other halves; even the part where homosexuality is explained.

"Ah, yes," he strokes his beard. He poses professorially. Despite the fact that we are in my office, I feel like a captured coed. I feel like that college impostor; the girl who whored her way into the hallowed halls of academia. I feel sick.

"Excuse me," I say, getting tangled in his legs as I escape down the hall and into the office-sized women's room.

Startled, or perhaps distracted with more enticing noon plans, Bob disappears from my lunch ritual. I am unpleasantly surprised to notice that I notice his absence. I do not finish my cream cheese sandwich but pick out the sliced olives and eat them. I begin to wonder what it would be like to go to bed with Bob; to go to bed with a man not for money. Cecile has done this. She has not ever told me about it, but she has told me about being married. Married only for a few months and to a gay man, but married is married; married is fucked.

To stop my own stupid thoughts, I take a slug of cold coffee and walk out of my office. My coworkers—the people I supervise—silence themselves when they see me. It is Friday and the office talk has been of weekend plans and lottery fantasies. Now there is only the barking of computer keyboards; the futuristic blur of incoming phone calls; the modulated voices used for citizens. I bring another Styrofoam cup of coffee back to my cubicle. Sounds rush behind me, as if I were walking away from the ocean suddenly alive with a storm.

I sip more coffee.

My stomach is killing me, but still I sip more coffee.

I look over a monthly report. Last month's.

I decide I should clean my ceramic cups, but do not want to part the seas of my coworkers to get to the bathroom's running water.

When my phone rings with its special Cecile ring, I jump on it, but let it ring another time before I answer it.

But it is not Cecile, it is Maura.

"Cecile gave me your number," she says.

Well, I think, at least I was close.

"I need to see you. I've got an emergency."

"Come to the office," I say. I do not like Maura, remembering her from the Women's Coffeehouse. The smugness of women like Maura confounds me. Despite, or perhaps because of, those philosophy courses I took in college, I often engage in the fallacy of duality. There are two kinds of people in the world, I say. There are those who have money; and those who do not. Or there are those who drink coffee; and those who will not. Or there are those who have been married; and those who have not.

Or there are those who stood with their sandals slipping off the curb, listening to the smooth sound of a late model car as it slows and its power window glides down, peering inside to see what could be seen about danger and risk and price, and then answering the question "How much?"

And there are those who have never; never had to.

Like Maura.

But she's a dyke, and dyke is family, and family is help offered whenever it is needed.

Maura is a tarot card reader. Of course, so am I, but Maura dresses the part. She jangles into the office with her cotton pants that gather at the ankle and colored strings tied around her extremities and loops of silver through her ears and nose. She looks like a white and privileged child dressed up as a gypsy for Hallowe'en. My coworkers stare.

Maura delivers her problem in circles, concentric and dramatic. It sounds for a while as if she had been kidnapped by a car salesman from Dodge Country; then as if she had burned her to-be-traded car during the candle-and-incense farewell ritual. I listen, wondering if this is too insignificant to confide to her friend's lover, the politically correct attorney mentioned at the coffeehouse. I listen, assuming that she will explain the problem sooner or later.

She does. The title application lists her as the lienholder and Southeast Bank as the owner. She shows me a crumpled piece of paper. She cries, as if the whole universe has turned vice versa.

"Don't worry, Maura," I say, sounding like someone's mother; remembering that I am someone's mother. "The information was just input incorrectly. It's easy to fix."

I take her to a terminal, call up the file, switch Block A and Block B, print a revised title application. It takes about two minutes.

"I hate computers," she says. If Colby was standing there clutching that piece of paper, I would say "You're welcome" in that sarcastic tone that makes him quickly say "Thank you," acknowledging his forgotten manners. As a mother, it's my duty to instill consideration; my obligation to the family of dykes does not extend that far.

"I think I'll go put a hex on that place. Stupid salesman. Screwing up the title application like that." Now that there is no reason to be angry, Maura is angry.

"What about ethics?" I am suddenly hungry for an abstract conversation about the nature of things.

"Fuck ethics," Maura says.

"Besides," I add, "what could be a worse curse than being a used car salesman?"

I think this is funny, but I do not have a chance to laugh, because Maura laughs for me as she answers: "Being a supervisor at the Department of Motor Vehicles."

Division. It is the Division of Motor Vehicles. But I do not correct her as she walks down the hall. My coworkers smirk slightly, pretend to be fascinated with their terminals.

I think I'll have another cup of coffee.

I think I'll go and pick up Colby early.

I think I'll go home and try to talk with Cecile.

12:02 p.m.
Doris Vanderlipp Manley

briefcases
under armpits
hold lunches
instead of briefs

squashed egg salad
sandwiches
two cookies
a hundred calories apiece

fine leathers
zippered
alligator-ed
they look so couth
brown paper bags

they look so un

on being a bureaucrat in spring

Doris Vanderlipp Manley

you say to yourself
I am going to practice zen
and enjoy every minute
it is fun sitting here
clean and well dressed
exercising your brain cells

you should be reveling in
the fluorescent lights
the nice metal desk with
baked enamel finish
the swivel chair upholstered
in mustard yellow vinyl

but somehow
this shuffling of papers
from desk to desk
this locking away of living
things in filing cabinets
this posturing professional stance

is against nature

"CONTRA NATURAM" as the poet said
contra my desire to breathe free
contra my craving for sunshine
and the sparkle of green leaves
contra my need to be held by lovers

WHAT AM I DOING HERE?

why don't I jump up
rip the phone lines
out of the floor
write go fuck yourself
on the desk tops
and run out to the woods
laughing?

Adeste Fideles

Deborah Fruin

Ginseng: Drink it down and it will keep you up. Too oblique. *The Oriental elixir of love, Ginseng: Drink it down and it will keep you up.* Better. Patty soaped her face with a squirt of liquid from the pump above the sink, a pink detergent that reminded her in taste and viscosity of Dr. Respond's Joy Jel for which she had recently written the slick Jelabrate! ad campaign slated to appear as a four-color, gate-fold spread in the May issue of *Pink Panties.*

Quite a coup. Too bad it made Patty want to slash her wrists. She sloughed off the surface derma, imagining the snickers of derision that would accompany an *Ad Week* "Critique" of Jelabrate tear sheets, until she was distracted from her misery by a muffled churning. She turned off the tap to listen. The sound of tire chains on a snowy road, she'd swear it was, though last time she looked there was no snow in Hollywood. Maybe Santa's Helper? Since Thanksgiving a purse snatcher, or maybe a gang of them, had haunted the office buildings along Sunset Boulevard and one victim swore that before the robbery she had heard a distant metallic rattling, which she likened to sleigh bells, hence the holiday moniker Santa's Helper.

Patty was a statistical aberration, having lived four years in Los Angeles without mishap: her car had never been boosted; her apartment had never been ransacked; her person had never been violated. But it was Christmas at the close of the year when her life had turned from merely drab to degrading, so it seemed fitting that she would now be mugged in a public toilet while wearing only her underwear. She rinsed her face with hot water, dried it with a stiff brown paper towel, thinking if her luck did not change she was going to send Jelabrate to *Ad Week* and die of humiliation, the first suicide by shame.

"It's me." The ladies' room door slammed open and Sweetheart came in, shucking the long sweatshirt she wore as a dress before the metal door wheezed closed behind her. She was praying-mantis thin, but, unreasonably, Patty thought, still superbly built. She perched herself on the edge of the sink, braless, as unself-conscious as a wood nymph, and pulled a metal-pronged hairbrush from her bag.

"What are you wearing tonight?" Sweetheart asked. Patty pointed to the tangerine silk dress embalmed in dry cleaner's plastic hanging from the toilet stall door.

"I'd look like an orange Popsicle in that." Sweetheart shook out her waist-length, cognac-colored hair, brushing until it shone, her dozen bangle bracelets making a racket with each stroke. "You're lucky you've got the shape to fill it out. I'd look like a toothpick in a garbage bag."

"Well, thanks," Patty said. "I don't think you could have said anything that would have made me feel fatter."

"And I'm not kidding," Sweetheart said. "It's really beautiful."

Sweetheart was employed to answer the telephones, though it was a job for which she had no talent: She was good at welcoming callers with a warm, "Good morning, Upright," but she could not announce, transfer, or place calls without hang ups, disconnects, and hurt feelings. Her real job was to cook lunch for the boss on a hot plate in the coffee room, making eggs just the way he liked them, cooked to the consistency of curdled mucus. No one had ever seen for sure what else she prepared for him because, at once mesmerized and horrified, they could not tear their eyes away from the slippery mound of eggs.

"I hear someone's going to be fired tomorrow," Sweetheart said, digging through her canvas workout bag to find her party frock, a red leather miniskirt.

"How do you know this?" Patty asked, swabbing on under-eye cover-up with a square of toilet paper. Most employees believed that Sweetheart knew these things because she not only made Dexter's lunch, she fed it to him while straddling his lap.

"Well, first of all, Beverly is here," she said slipping into a skirt that looked child-sized or smaller, a wide belt or a red Ace bandage.

"Who?"

"Beverly. The woman crying at the typewriter. Clint's mistress. Bev-er-ly." Sweetheart repeated the woman's name syllabically as if explaining something painfully obvious to a slow learner. "She wants to go to Betty Ford, but Clint won't pay. He says her only problem is she's bored and she should work for a change. He wants her to work here, so my guess is somebody's gotta go." She pulled on a scarlet, sequined tube top and further flattened her chest with yards of hefty gold chain jewelry.

"Who?" Patty asked.

"I'm not sure," Sweetheart said, and with a lick of her lips she was out the door, not once having looked in the mirror. "See you there," she said, her miniskirted high spirits reverberating through the john.

Patty pretended nonchalance, but Sweetheart's news flash had struck a spark of hope in her, perhaps not even as bright as the light from a Kama Sutra Love Potion candle, but no matter how dim, its flame revealed a way out. If Dexter fired her, she could collect unemployment. That one hundred sixty-six bucks per week was all it would take to set her free. Patty had been meaning to quit ever since she realized that Dexter had lied when he hired her. She had left her job at *Caravan*, the bible of the travel-trailer trade, when Dexter told her he was "getting out of skin" and launching a consumer magazine along the lines of *People*. If Patty hopped on board, she'd be first in line as captain of the new mag. Meanwhile, he would double her *Caravan* salary. Ahoy, matey. Patty thought her ship had come in, but it soon became clear that at Upright she would never write anything but gutter swill about sex contraptions. By that time, though, Patty had contracted paycheck inertia, too ragged after working nine to five to polish her resume, scour the classifieds, and surely she could not be expected to network after a day at Upright. Her rent was paid but her life was over.

Patty applied buff-colored foundation with a damp sponge. The rhythm of the ad copy she was working on fused with the carols piped into the john: *Raindrops on roses and spike heels with net hose. Lift bras of black lace and whiskers on kittens...and feathery French ticklers...Bright colored condoms come five to a pack...try them and like them or get money back!* The more Patty thought about it, the more obvious it became that hers was a job Dexter's girlfriend would be good at since sobriety was not a requirement. Indeed, it could be a handicap.

Deidre Evans replaced Sweetheart at the second sink. She was the design mind behind the photo shoots and ad layouts and called herself the "Diana Vreeland of Sleaze." With a five-year tenure, Deidre was an Upright lifer who had once, in a frantic bid for expulsion, released a *Pink Panties* cover featuring the female genitalia in medical textbook detail, but photographed in such an artful way that the cover made it all the way to the newsstands uncensored and there discovered, soon created a sensation. The publicity doubled *Pink Panties'* sales and in gratitude Dexter tripled Deidre's salary, making her a virtual prisoner at Upright.

"I just saw Sweetheart coming out of here."

"Yes," Patty said. "She'd be hard to miss. My Christmas stocking has more fabric in it than her party dress."

"Just don't underestimate her, if you get my meaning," Deidre said.

Patty stood soldierlike and forlorn in front of the mirror not having the slightest idea what Deidre's meaning was. Was Deidre reprimanding her for a lack of sisterly compassion? Or had Sweetheart already told Deidre who would be fired tomorrow? Was Deidre warning Patty not to believe everything Sweetheart said? Patty watched Deidre apply rosy moisturizer, leaning into the mirror for a critical appraisal. What, Patty pondered, was her point?

"Why do they always use green tiles and fluorescent lights in public rest rooms?" Patty complained. "It's dispiriting."

"It's designed to be," Deidre said, running a slate-grey eyeliner pencil around her green eyes. "It's psychological manipulation meant to leave you feeling grotesque and powerless."

"What color is that eyeliner?"

"Mysterioso," Deidre said, her lips a taut O, cheeks hollowed to receive a wee bit of contour, a splotch of blush.

"It's very subtle," Patty said, studying Deidre's mirror image.

"Blondes can't carry off primary colors, too overpowering," Deidre said, her eyes meeting Patty's in the mirror. "Of course, some of us are more suited to bold strokes. Blue at the eyes, red at the lips works for you, lucky girl."

Patty looked in the mirror and pulled a brush through her corn-yellow hair, setting it on end with static electricity.

"Bozo," she said.

"What?" Deidre stopped painting.

"I said I don't want to go," Patty said, pulling mascara from her makeup bag.

"Desire has nothing to do with it. The Upright, Inc. Christmas party is a command performance. Clint's going to buy you dinner, darling. Surely you can choke it down."

Patty doubted it.

"Who was that woman sitting outside your cubicle this afternoon? Orange hair; cockeyed ponytail." Deidre made a fist and stuck it to the side of her head where the ponytail had been. "White parachute-silk jump suit. Loud weeping."

"That's Beverly, Dexter's mistress," Patty said.

"Well, I've never seen her before."

"She wants to go to Betty Ford, but it's too expensive so Dexter wants her to work here."

"Doing what?"

"Somebody else's job. Sweetheart says someone is getting fired tomorrow," Patty said.

"No!" Deidre's Lipshaper wand clattered into the sink convincing Patty she had been taken by surprise. "It could be me, you know," Deidre said. "I've done a stinking job lately. Though I doubt that matters." She had not abandoned all hope, Patty noted. "Still," Deidre closed her eyes as if in prayer, "Santa, I just want you to know, I wouldn't ask for another single thing if I could have this, but act now because this offer is only good until 6:00 p.m. this evening." Deidre opened her eyes and gazed into the mirror as if it were a streaked and water-spotted crystal ball in which she could grimly review the past. "Last year Dexter handed out envelopes at the restaurant. Our 'bonuses' were drink chits. We each got two. A Christmas party with a no-host bar. Never again. I'd draw the line." Deidre drew a wet line along the rim of the sink, but it was a flimsy thing that could not separate her from Upright, Inc. and Clint Dexter.

"Who do you think it will be?" Patty asked.

"So, you want a parole for the holidays, too," Deidre said, giving Patty the Mysterioso eye. "You're responsible for the Jelabrate campaign, aren't you? That might have been a fatal mistake." Deidre bent at the waist, working styling mousse into her root ends. "I think it's going to be Trinka."

"No!" Patty protested. "Not even Dexter could do that. She's the only one he never screams at."

"She's a rabbit. She sits in his office, her little bunny paws folded on her fluffy bunny knees, squirming on her cotton tail. Whiskers twitching." Deidre made a rabbity face at herself in the mirror and wiggled her behind. "Dexter hates her."

"Dexter hates everybody."

"Yeah, but he thinks the rest of us deserve it. Her purity shows him off for the petty tyrant he is."

Clint Dexter was routinely despised by all who worked for him. "Brauuggh!" he screamed when you walked into his office. "You're trying to ruin me!" Unlikely. No one at Upright, Inc. performed with sufficient enthusiasm to ruin anyone but themselves. As far as Patty could tell, everyone stuck predictably close to the sordid conventions of pornographic mail order. Many of her coworkers had families or expensive drug habits to support and could not play fast and loose with the paycheck Dexter doled out.

Besides, ruin Dexter? Impossible. It would be easier to kill him. He already suffered from numerous vague but debilitating illnesses and chronic conditions: a constant fatigue that laid him low by 1:30 every afternoon; a bloody bowel condition that turned his insides to beet juice and made him occasionally cough up a fine mist of blood, sometimes leaving faint traces on copy pages or ad paste ups; an untreatable lower lumbar problem that every few months nailed him to his office sofa, a quivering bug on a pin, depending on Sweetheart to wheel him to and from his car via a gurney, issuing orders as he rolled through departments. There were the migraines, and the recurring scaly skin condition, something between shingles and psoriasis, that he claimed was the most agonizing affliction of them all. And one day he suffered what appeared to be a minor stroke right in the middle of one of his "You're-out-to-destroy-me" fist-shaking sessions. "Who are you people?" he demanded. Then there was some stupendous confusion, and for a while everyone thought this might be it, cerebral shutdown that was medically certifiable, but his brush with brain death only made him ornerier.

"Oh my god, you're right." Patty swallowed the fact that Trinka was the most likely to be fired. "But it's not fair. I've been here seven months longer than she has. I deserve to go first. I will go first."

"I understand how you feel, kid," Deidre said slipping into a pair of gold stiletto heels, "but what are you going to do about it?"

"Whatever I have to," Patty said ripping the plastic tissue off her tangerine silk.

Trinka looked miserable in her red party dress, a woebegone snowman hanging onto the white lace collar for dear life. Patty had wracked her brain for a way to keep Trinka in and get herself out of Upright, but the only thing she came up with was a confrontation that started out with, "Listen, girly," and ended with a threat.

"You look very pretty tonight, Trinka."

"So do you, Patty. Thanks for being my date."

"I'm sure you'd much rather be going with your husband," Patty said. "But as the boss says, 'I haven't stayed in business forty years by feeding freeloaders'."

"It doesn't really matter. It doesn't seem much like Christmas to me," she said, locking herself into a toilet stall, a pair of glitter panty hose in her hand.

"What? This doesn't seem Christmasy to you?" Patty said. "What could be more seasonal? L.A.'s showing off its best colors, blood red and U.S. Treasury green. I suppose you're from a mistletoe and holly kind of place?"

"Thurston, Minnesota. My husband warned me. He said I shouldn't get my heart set on an old-fashioned Christmas. He thought a tree and all that would just make me more homesick, but we went ahead and got one anyway. A small one. I'm sure that kind of stuff doesn't matter to you. L.A. is your home, but I can't get used to it."

"Actually, I'm from Oregon, Illinois. Pop. 3800."

"I don't believe it!" Trinka said, emerging from the stall with her new stockings on, feet plugged into patent leather flats, toes aflutter with taffeta bows, she looked ready to carry a candle in the Bethlehem

84

Lutheran Christmas pageant back home. "You seem, I don't know, so big city."

Patty wondered if Trinka meant bitchy, but couldn't bring herself to say it?

"I'll prove it." Patty pulled her wallet out of her purse, "I still have my Oregon library card. And right next to it there, that's a picture of our farm." She handed the picture to Trinka, hoping to instill a black-earth-and-red-barn bond, convince the girl to trust her. "Keep your friends close and your enemies closer," Patty's daddy always said.

"I sure do miss home," Trinka said wistfully. "Especially at this time of year. I'm a nut about Christmas. When I was a little girl I believed I could remember heaven, from before I was born. It was silvery-pink with gilt-edged clouds and harp-strumming angels. My mom tried to set me straight, digging out the Christmas tree ornaments in the middle of July. 'See this,' she said, 'doesn't she look exactly like the angels you're talking about?' 'Yes!' I said. 'That's exactly what they looked like'." Trinka giggled. "To tell you the truth, I still think Christmastime is a little taste of heaven here on earth."

Ick! Patty felt herself slipping into sugar shock, as though she had been force-fed a pan of divinity.

"We might have been home for Christmas if I hadn't gotten this job. We promised to give California every chance. Four months ago we were both out of work and we almost had our bags packed when I got this job. It seemed like a stroke of luck, but it didn't turn out exactly as Mr. Dexter said it would."

Oh, grow up, Snow White. Patty had not given it much thought before, but now she realized that she, too, loathed the saccharine vulnerability that had made Trinka so reprehensible to Dexter. She felt utterly justified in her plan to beat Trinka to the unemployment office. The kid definitely needed a double shot of reality before climbing back into the Thurston womb.

Trinka turned on the tap and began to brush her teeth, working up a foam worthy of a hydrophobic cocker spaniel, a tiny flurry of Crest bubbles icing Frosty's black top hat, and in a momentary déjà vu, Patty saw in Trinka a reflection of herself not so many years before. She had graduated from State in June but didn't leave home until January because she wanted to be home for the holidays. Patty remembered her mother's gentle warning before she boarded the plane: "Be careful of your ambition, child, or it may turn you into the kind of person fit only to despise." Now here it was only a few short Christmases since and she had already surpassed her mother's worst fears. Patty took a hard look in the mirror and knew a change was long overdue.

"Do you hear what I hear? Jingle bells?" Trinka asked, her baby-bare eyes opened wide. "Oh, Patty, would you go see? Just the thought of that Santa's Helper scares me."

Patty hadn't heard, but to ease Trinka's mind she tiptoed over to the door and pulled it open a sliver. Up the hall, nothing. Down the hall she saw the backsides of Deidre and Sweetheart waltzing off together toward the elevator, Sweetheart's bangles and chains clanking against her bony frame. No ghosts, no muggers, a good omen.

"It's nothing," Patty said grabbing her folded office outfit and zipping up her purse. "Come on, let's get going." And she began to sing:

O come all ye faithful, drunken and rambunctious.
Oh come ye, oh come ye, to Woo Hong's restaurant.
Come and behold him, porno king par excellence...

"Patty! That's not the way the song goes," Trinka said in a tone of voice that suggested a reprimand.

"You're right, Trinka," Patty said pleased at herself for feeling a twinge of shame. "Let's sing it the right way." And they did, all the way to Woo Hong's.

Patty was still humming on her way home, performing a private postmortem of the party, which from her new outlook had gone pretty well. Trinka would be home for Christmas, that much seemed sure. Patty, determined to follow through on her early new year's resolution to get out of Upright on her own, pulled into a AM/PM to pick up the morning paper and vowed to read the classifieds that very night. It wasn't until she reached the checkout counter, festive with foil-dressed Santas and cellophane-wrapped candy canes, that she realized she'd been robbed.

Message to Network Users

Jean Flanagan

We are going to wire you
in to the multiplexor
on-line with us.
You'll be a bit slower
but no one will notice
not even you.
The compiler will give you
a choice of languages to speak.
Basic is basic
and of course you know Pascal.

Now login to the network.
Don't worry about syntax,
ambiguous verbs or invalid parameters.
Change your password
now and then so
no one is tempted
to use you
unauthorized.
Don't be idle,
log us out if
you think you might.
It slows us down,
slows up output.

Remember, keep us
within your buffers
and your jobs.
Warning: Chaos will get you
to bitnet and then
on to gateway.
Batch when you can
and purge every day
without fail.

Experienced Only Need Apply

Savina A. Roxas

October, 1935, was not the time to look for a job, or so Papa kept telling Mary. But all the Bronx could think of or talk about was the Recovery — the WPA jobs, thousands of them, skilled and unskilled, for people on Home Relief. Even Charles Soloman, the WEVD Socialist commentator, admitted that unemployment had taken a breather. Retail sales were up, new cars multiplied on the assembly lines: Mary believed the radio news.

Not Papa. "See," he'd say, spreading the *New York Times* across the kitchen table and wetting his finger on his tongue to turn the pages. "Situations Wanted by unemployed stenographers, columns of them." Then he'd count aloud the number of "Help Wanted, Female" ads. "Nine," he'd say. "Experienced only need apply." Convinced it was no use, Mary decided to give up trying. But the next morning, compulsively, she turned to the want ads. With a jolt she realized there was something different about the last ad in the column, the seventh one down:

> Clerical and typist; act as relief operator, plug switchboard, must be tireless worker, good personality. WILL TRAIN. No experience required. $5.00. Moe Levy & Son, 949 Broadway (23rd Street).

She traced *No experience required* on the palm of her hand like one of the kids getting ready to cheat on a test. Aloud, she said, "Wait till I tell Papa."

That night, when she heard Papa's key in the door, she quickly turned off the radio. Before he even had a foot in the hallway, she ran to him and said, "Papa, I'll take your things. Listen to the ad I found in the *Times* today."

He came in and brushed past her. She followed him. He said, "Let me catch my breath. Those five flights are murder." Then he gave her his hat and coat and disappeared into the bathroom. Dropping his things on the chair in the living room, she went into the kitchen, and walked around the kitchen table until he finally came in. His eyes avoided hers and she noticed that his lips were narrow and turned down at the corners. At the stove he raised the lid on the pots and said, "Looks good. Garlic brings out the taste in spinach."

Mary held up the copy of the ad, began to recite, "Clerical and typist..."

Papa interrupted, "I'm hungry. Let's eat."

"It won't take a minute," she pleaded.

"Later," he said, in a tone she knew well and obeyed.

Her brothers came to the table talking about the Chicago win. Frank suggested betting on tomorrow's game. Papa turned the radio on to the Buck Rogers program, and that stopped all the talk. To the radio's blare about adventures in space in the 21st century, they did a disappearing act with the spinach, eggs, bread, and milk. By the time Mary cleared off the dishes and put the apples and coffee out, "Amos 'n' Andy" was on. Mary knew better than to interrupt the Kingfish. Finally the program ended.

Mary wiped her hands dry on the front of her skirt and put the copy of the ad on the table in front of him. She sat down, clenched her hands in her lap. "Papa. Can you believe it? No experience required."

She watched the frown on his face deepen as he read. With a hiss in his voice he said, "It's a gyp. Look at that salary."

To the tune of "When the moon comes over the mountain...," Mary pressed her nails into the palm of her hand. "Oh, Papa. I'd get some experience. That's what I need."

"Twenty-third Street," he slurred, shaking his head. "A bad neighborhood. You'll get experience all right. Not the kind you need."

"But, Papa," she hurried to say. "It's Broadway and 23rd."

"So what?" he came back. "Down there it's not the Great White Way. The louses of the world hang out there."

"I knew you'd find something wrong," she said and stood up to back away from him. "I want to try." Her chin came forward. "Papa I'm going to try." She couldn't bear to listen to him exaggerating just to keep her home.

He paced up and down in front of the window, his eyes raised to the ceiling. "Stop. Go if you want to. You're giving me indigestion."

Papa had told her to get off the subway at the Fourteenth Street station, walk crosstown to Broadway, then uptown to 23rd Street. Money was short, so he gave her two nickels, one to go down and one to come home.

Her feet hurt horribly as she walked in high heels from 14th to 23rd. In front of the building at 949 Broadway a long double line of women snaked up the street as though it never ended. The ad. Oh, god! Could she be mistaken? Walking to the end of the line on 25th Street, she felt too embarrassed not to join the rest. More and more women lined up behind her. Bewildered, she wasn't sure of what to do. But when the blonde in front of her said this was the last time she'd answer an ad, Mary felt it was hopeless to stay.

She screwed up her courage and left the line not sure what to do. Aimlessly she headed uptown toward 42nd Street. It haunted her that she was losing her skills; three months now since she'd taken dictation from Mr. Bruce, who stood in front of the class in a stiff white collar and funny rimless glasses that pinched the bridge of his nose. She'd have to find some way to practice. Remembering the "Instruction, Female" section of the want ads, she went into the 42nd Street Library to look up the *Times*. From the many ads she chose the Miller Institute of Shorthand at 1450 Broadway: "Refresher course in exchange for morning work."

The receptionist on the fifth floor looked over the application form Mary had filled out. "Your name looks Italian. I just got a call from the Braden Advertising Agency. They want someone who knows enough Italian to type a LaRosa Macaroni radio script. Can you do it?"

"Sure. I speak nothing else at home. Where do I go?"

"Here's the address and carfare. We don't pay you for working, but we supply carfare. I'll call the agency and say you're on the way. Take the local subway to 68th Street. Then walk down to Riverside Drive."

Mary picked up the slip of paper with the address. "I'll be back tomorrow for my practice?"

"Yes. We're flexible. Come in any time."

At the Braden Advertising Agency, Mrs. Braden, short and quite heavy, greeted Mary at the door and ushered her to the typing area.

"Here's a model of the script form I want you to follow," Mrs. Braden said. "If you have any questions don't hesitate to come to me." Mary went to the desk near the window and typed from an Italian longhand original. Without looking up once, she typed until the job was done. Then she proofed it the way Mr. Bruce said to do it: one line at a time reading aloud. Not finding any mistakes, she brought the script to Mrs. Braden who was sitting on a couch with her feet curled under her. Scanning the pages, she said, "Good work, Mary. LaRosa is one of our new accounts. We really need someone who knows Italian. Come back tomorrow. There's more work for you to do." She stood up and walked Mary to the door and said, "By the way Mary, that's a handsome suit you're wearing. It looks custom made."

"Thank you," Mary said. "My father's a custom tailor. He makes all my clothes. Is nine o'clock tomorrow morning OK?"

"Yes." Mrs. Braden answered. "I'll expect you."

At home Mary waited impatiently to tell Papa the good news. When she heard his key in the door, instead of running to him, she sat in the kitchen chair and waited. He came in, looked at her, his face pale. He made no attempt to take off his hat and coat, "What happened?" he asked hoarsely.

Softly and calmly she said, "I got a job. No pay. But the kind of experience that will get me one that pays."

"What are you talking about?" he shrieked. "23rd Street? No pay?"

"No. Not there," she said. And slowly she let it spill from her tongue that it was on Riverside Drive.

"How fancy! Riverside Drive? What's on Riverside Drive?" He took off his hat, wiped his forehead with the back of his hand.

All in a rush, now, she told him about the long line, the blonde, the Miller Institute, and the Braden Advertising Agency. "And, Papa, Mrs. Braden liked my suit. She knew right away it was custom made."

"Naturally she liked it. I haven't been a tailor all these years for nothing. But, no pay, what a gyp," he shook his hands wildly in protest. "If I were you . . ."

"Papa we're missing Buck Rogers."

He took off his coat and put it on the chair. "Yeah, he's in the new spaceship. Let's hear if he does as well as you did today." He reached over, snapped on the radio, and there was no more talk about gyps. She heard a spaceship zap by with a staccato sound like gunfire. After a while, she didn't hear it. She just heard the hum of success in the air.

Woman Sitting at the Machine, Thinking

Karen Brodine

Excerpt from a Series of Work Poems

she thinks about everything at once without making a mistake.
no one has figured out how to keep her from doing this thinking
while her hands and nerves also perform every complex
function of the work. this is not automatic or deadening.
try it sometime. make your hands move quickly on the keys
fast as you can, while you are thinking about:

the layers, fossils. the idea that this machine she controls
is simply layers of human workhours frozen in steel, tangled
in tiny circuits, blinking out through lights like hot, red eyes.
the noise of the machine they all sometimes wig out to, giddy,
zinging through the shut-in space, blithering atoms;
everyone's hands paused midair above the keys
while Neil or Barbara solo, wrists telling every little thing,
feet blipping along, shoulders raggly.

she had always thought of money as solid, stopped.
but seeing it as moving labor, human hours, why that means
it comes back down to her hands on the keys, shoulder aching,
brain pushing words through fingers through keys, trooping
out crisp black ants on the galleys. work compressed into
instruments, slim computers, thin as mirrors, how could
numbers multiply or disappear, squeezed in sideways like that
but they could, they did, obedient and elegant, how amazing.
the woman whips out a compact, computes the cost,
her face shining back from the silver case
her fingers, sharp tacks, calling up the digits.

when she sits at the machine, rays from the cathode stream
directly into her chest. when she worked as a clerk, the rays
from the xerox angled upward, striking her under the chin.
when she waited tables the micro oven sat at stomach level.
when she typeset for Safeway, dipping her hands in processor
chemicals, her hands burned and peeled and her chest ached
from the fumes.

well we know who makes everything we use or can't use.
as the world piles itself up on the bones of the years,
so our labor gathers.

while we sell ourselves in fractions. they don't want us all
at once, but hour by hour, piece by piece. our hands mainly
and our backs. and chunks of our brains. and veiled expressions
on our faces, they buy. though they can't know what actual
thoughts stand behind our eyes.

then they toss the body out on the sidewalk at noon and at five.
then they spit the body out the door at sixty-five.

each morning:

fresh thermos of coffee at hand; for the slowing down, shift
gears, unscrew the lid of the orange thermos, pour out a whiff
of home, morning paper, early light. a tangible pleasure
against the unlively words.

funny, though. this set of codes slips through my hands, a
loose grid of shadows with big gaps my own thoughts sneak
through . . .

call format o five. Reports Disc 2, quad left
return. name of town, address, zip. quad left
return. rollalong and there you are.
done with this one. start the next.

call format o five. my day so silent yet taken up with words.
floating through the currents and cords of my wrists
into the screen and drifting to land, beached pollywogs.
all this language handled yet the room is so silent.
everyone absorbed in feeding words through the machines.

enter file execute.

call file Oceana. name of town, Pacifica. name of street, Arbor.
thinking about lovemaking last night, how it's another land,
another set of sounds, the surface of the water, submerged,
then floating free, the delicate fabric of motion and touch
knit with listening and humming and soaring.

never a clear separation of power because it is both our power
at once. hers to speak deep in her body and voice to her own
rhythms. mine to ride those rhythms out and my own,
and call them out even more. a speaking together from body
to mouth to voice.

replace file Oceana.
call file Island.

scroll up....................scroll down.
what is there to justify?

the words gliding on the screen like the seal at the aquarium,
funny whiskers, old man seal, zooming by upside down
smirking at the crowd, mocking us
and his friends the dolphins, each sharp black and cream marking
streamlined as the water

huh. ugh, they want this over and over:
MAY 1 MAY 1 MAY 1 MAY 1 MAY 1 enough?
MAY 1 MAY 1

once I have typeset all the pages, I run the job out on tape
and clip it to the videosetter to be punched out.
then I swing out the door to get another job.

down the stairs into the cramped room where Mary and Rosie
and Agnes sit in the limp draft of one fan.
"must be 95 in here." "yeah, and freezing in the other room."
"got to keep the computers cool, you know."

back up the stairs past management barricaded
behind their big desks on the way to everything.
on the way to the candy machine.
on the way to the bathroom.
on the way to lunch.
I pretend they are invisible.
I pretend they have great big elephant ears.

and because they must think we are stupid in order
to push us around, *they* become stupid.
knowing "something's going on," peering like moles.
how can they know the quirk of an eyebrow behind their back?
they suspect we hate them because they know
what they are doing to us—but we are only
stupid Blacks or crazy Puerto Ricans, or dumb blonds.

we are their allergy, their bad dream.
they need us too much, with their talk of
"carrying us" on the payroll.
we carry them, loads of heavy dull metal,
outmoded and dusty.

98

they try to control us, building partitions,
and taking the faces off the phones.
they talk to us slow and loud,
HOW ARE YOU TODAY? HERE'S A CHECK FOR YOU.
As if it were a gift.

we say — even if they stretched tape
across our mouths
we could still speak to one another
with our eyebrows.

Machines
Karen Loeb

This kitchen table is my outpost, my place to wait and worry about Pamela. I won't feel right till she's home. She's only over at her friend Angie's house, but still, she has to walk home, and anything could happen. She doesn't know about dangers on the streets. I tell her to be home before dark, but she won't listen to me anymore. I keep meaning to have her hearing checked. I really think something could be wrong with it. God knows, I have slaved for my kids. What the hell do they think I go to work every day for? For my health? God. And I thought I worked hard when I was a clerk in the bookshop before I met Cliff. Nothing compares to those horrible machines I work on morning to night. And Hank had the nerve to say to me, right before he went to Viet Nam, that I wasn't working for *him*. After all, *he* lived with Cliff. Did he really think that Cliff bought him all those clothes and paid for his first year of college?

Those machines. They have more keys than twenty grand pianos. When I first started in the bank, I was slow. I was always pressing the wrong column keys, and my supervisor Opal was always coming over and canceling out my procedure. I must have called her over a hundred times my first day on the job. They just put me on this big machine and said to post these accounts. God. They were stacked to the goddamn ceiling. And every one of them had to be right. You know how people scrutinize their bank statements. And if there's one thing wrong, those goddamned customers call up the minute it arrives, or worse yet they come in and the guard sends them upstairs to the bookkeeping department. And if it's a mistake you made, Opal makes you talk to the customer. Every account is coded so we can tell who posted it. God.

My second week there, I'm sitting behind my machine. It's so tall, I can't see over it. All I can see are the keys and the women sitting at machines to either side. We all smoke, thank god. I don't know what I would do if I couldn't smoke. Sometimes I smoke thirty cigarettes at work. I used to only smoke a pack a day when I wasn't working. But now I smoke thirty at work, and that doesn't count the ones I smoke in the morning and the ones at night when I come home so dead I could drop in the middle of the kitchen floor, but instead, I have to do the goddamned breakfast dishes because Pamela can't even do that for me. She can't even wash the breakfast dishes. And then I have to figure out something to eat for the both of us, and after dinner I do one chore, like washing the kitchen floor or cleaning the stove, but sometimes I'm so tired, I just go up to bed right after dinner. I crawl into bed and read until I fall asleep. I fall asleep with my light burning right in my eyes, that's how tired I am. Those bastards at work really wring it out of you.

It was only my second week of work and I hear that silver bell ring on the counter. All of us hate to hear that sound, because it always means trouble. It means that a customer is there wanting something. No one who works in the bank rings the bell — they're allowed to walk behind the counter and look things up themselves. "Oh, Iris," Opal calls. She's Southern, and her words slide off her tongue like a snake. Each word is twice as long as it really is the way she says it. She has black hair that everyone says she dyes and I know she dyes. It's just too black to believe. They say she went grey when she was twenty. I've heard of things like that. In fact, Pamela has a girlfriend at teachers' college whose hair is grey. I almost forgot about that. It's pretty amazing to see a young person with grey hair. Opal has big breasts too, and she doesn't hide them. She wore tight clothes. She couldn't wait for winter so she could pull out the sweaters and saunter around. She didn't hire me. I was sent to her department from personnel. The personnel director said he thought I was a very nice lady, and he's sure I would fit in wherever they placed me in the bank, and he knew of an opening in bookkeeping. I started at $400 a month because I didn't have experience. I was one of the oldest ones in my department. Most of the rest of them were young girls out of high school who were biding their time until the right man came along. I wanted to tell them that there was no right man, but I guess they'll have to find that out for themselves. I thought I had the right man too, and twenty-five years later, I'm pounding a goddamned machine.

"Yes, Opal," I said, from behind my machine, when she drawled out my name.

"Customer wants you."

I could feel JoAnn and Helen watching me as I finished my transaction and pushed back my chair. I took a good drag on my cigarette. I wasn't going to let it go to waste. And I stood up. Opal was standing on our side of the counter tapping her long frosty white fingernails, and a man in a cashmere overcoat with a balding head was standing on the other side. I could tell right away I was dealing with class. These people I work with don't understand anything about class. They speak some perverted form of English. Wouldn't they be surprised to know that I went to the University of Chicago? But I could tell that this man spoke the King's English. He was a little pudgy, well a lot pudgy—he wasn't my type. If I'm ever going to marry again, I want to find a man who isn't bald and isn't fat, but there aren't many of them walking around in my age bracket. God. But why the hell shouldn't I be choosy? I mean, I have to sleep with the person, don't I? I just couldn't stand it if he were bald. For all Cliff's faults, he still has his hair, I will say that, though I noticed the last time he came over to have dinner with Pamela that his hairline seems to be receding a little. Well, I don't have to put up with that. Not any more. That bitch Delilah he's involved with does. She has to lie down with a balding man. But not me. I guess Hank will be bald. They say if your mother's brothers go bald, you will, speaking from Hank's standpoint. Well two of my brothers are practically like Yul Brynner, so I guess Hank will be too, if that's a correct theory.

I walk between the machines and over to where Opal is standing. She smiles at me, showing her chipped tooth. She thinks she is the cat's meow, and then she smiles. She doesn't know how unattractive that chipped tooth makes her look. From what I understand, most of the teeth in her mouth aren't hers, and that's why she hangs on to this chipped tooth, like it's a big deal or something. "Iris," she says, "this is Mr. McKinley. He's having some problems figuring out his account. Won't you help him?" She smiled so sweetly, not at me, but at him, blinking her eyes. Then she walked away. I had never waited on a customer — it was only my second week, and it was just my luck that statements went out when I started working there.

"I think there's a mistake on my statement," the man said. He unfolded the green paper. I got a little shiver watching him do it, because his nails were all dirty underneath. Here he was dressed in a $300 dollar coat, and his nails were dirty. Ugh. That's worse than bald. I can't imagine letting someone touch me whose nails are dirty. One thing about Cliff, his nails were always clean.

"Well, just let me see the statement, sir," I said.

He held the statement to his chest. I wasn't going to reach out and grab it from him, if that's what he thought. He clutched that damn thing and leaned over to me. Then that bastard hissed out, "This statement is all fucked up. What the fuck are you going to do about it, girlie?"

My hands and feet went icy. I could feel antennae go up all over the room. Everyone's ears seemed to grow. I stood there wanting to cry. I mean, I had a choice between working on that bookkeeping machine or talking with this bastard. I felt a whoosh of air and Opal was by my side. "Is there some kind of problem, Mr. McKinley?" she said.

"My statement . . ."

"Perhaps you should take it up with our vice president. He's standing right over there. I'll call him over."

Before Mr. McKinley could agree, she waved over Mr. Barnaby and gave him some kind of high sign. After they left, JoAnn and Helen who sit on either side of me came over to the counter. "No one can talk to us like that," Opal stated. "The minute a customer swears, we don't got to handle it." She squinted at us. After she stood up for me, I still thought she was a brassy washed-out woman, but I admired her some even though she murders the English language.

Helen is a Greek lady who was always bringing pastries to work from her husband's restaurant. JoAnn had been in the bookkeeping department longer than anyone. She lives with her son. When her son was four, her husband molested him. God. What a class of people. And besides that, JoAnn's last name is Hooker. How much bad luck can a person have? Helen and JoAnn smoked Marlboro filters and I constantly had to pass the packs back and forth. I didn't know why they didn't just put the two of them next to each other. When I suggested it once, Opal told me to mind my own business, that there was one boss in the department and was I aware of who it was? Myself, I smoke Kools. They don't have those silly white filters on the tip. Pamela used to love to save the empty packs because of the picture of the penguin. It's the menthol that gives it the name Kool. They put menthol in cough drops to make your throat feel better, so they can't be all bad. Helen and JoAnn are older than most of the women here, but they're still years younger than I am. I don't know how I got so old so fast.

It was one of the darkest days of my life, the first time I got fired from a bank job. Almost as dark as when my mother died, and when my final divorce papers arrived in the mail, and when Hank went to live with Cliff, and when Cliff married Delilah and my sister Claudia came to spend the whole day and night because I didn't think I could go on because that bitch Delilah had been a friend and teacher of mine, but that's a different story.

I had been pounding away on that goddamned machine for nine months. I was able to process almost a thousand checks a day. My god. A thousand checks. When Opal calls me over to her desk. Just like that. She tells me that I had really made good progress for someone who had absolutely no experience. I thought she was going to offer me a raise. I hadn't gotten one yet. Instead she says that even though I made progress, it wasn't enough. That they needed someone who could do at least two thousand checks a day. But I had the least number of errors of anyone, I said. That didn't matter, she said. They wanted someone who could produce. God. I sat there, thinking of my mortgage payment and how I had to go grocery shopping on Saturday and how the child support payment had already been spent on the stack of bills that were almost past due when I paid them. Plus, I felt like a failure. I mean, I don't think I knew another person who could stand to work this machine. I thought of my sister Claudia, who has enough trouble climbing up on a bus with her crooked little body. There weren't many people in the world who could work these machines. I thought I had accomplished something. Even though it wasn't something I wanted to accomplish, I had done it, nevertheless. And here this twerp was telling me that I wasn't fast enough. She was young enough to be my daughter. But I was glad she wasn't. I have enough trouble with Pamela and her mouth.

I went home that afternoon and wondered what I was going to do. How I was going to keep the house and what would become of Pamela and me. I knew that Hank would be OK because he was living with Cliff. That was what was arranged after the split-up. But I sat in the kitchen, right here where I'm sitting now, except that was eight years ago and we had a round table and now we have a card table that's square. I was sitting right by the wall phone, and I knew Claudia would be home from teaching, but I didn't have the nerve to call her. Pamela was over at a friend's house. I always know where Pamela is. I told her she could go visit anyone she wanted as long as she told me where she was going. No one can blame me for that. She's been carrying a key to this house ever since we moved in here when she was ten and had to let herself in after school. God. I used to agonize over her being here alone for two hours before I came home from work. But the day I got fired I was home early. I pounded my fist on the table. Why the hell did I have to buy such a big house? The payment was $115 a month. I know some people didn't consider that much, but it was all I could do to pay it, and now I didn't have an income. God. The house has a full basement and attic and two floors in between. I only wanted four bedrooms so we could rent one out to a boarder and have one for Hank when he stayed over. It didn't seem like so much when I bought it. But we've never had a boarder. And a double living room and a formal dining room didn't seem too extravagant. You have to eat somewhere. It's true we always eat in the kitchen except when company comes. And it's true, I haven't been able to do upkeep on the house. I had it painted when we first moved in. $600. God. The house is so tall they had to use scaffolding. And the $600 was just for the outside. They did the whole inside too. I just couldn't stand that cabbage flower wallpaper. It was all over the downstairs, like a bad dream every time I looked at the walls, which was all the time, because how can you be in a room and not look at the walls? It took three coats to cover those flowers too. Well, I know the house needs painting. Ten years later and it still hasn't been repainted on the outside. Five years ago I hired a man to scrape and paint the front so it wouldn't look so bad.

Then I was lying in bed one night with the window open. It was still light out. It stays light till nine o'clock. I don't remember it doing that in Chicago in the old days, but it does now. And this man and his wife walked by. I know because they stopped and had a conversation right on my sidewalk. They were staring up at the house. I could just feel them doing it. And the man said, "Now why do you suppose they didn't have the whole thing painted? It looks so sloppy this way." His wife said, "Oh, you know, dear, some people have odd notions about things." I wanted to scream down, "It's the best I could do—I didn't have the money to paint the whole thing. It would have been a thousand dollars." Maybe I should have asked them for the money. I lay in bed and clutched the sheet and I cried because I wished I did have the money to do the whole thing.

How could I not buy a house? Pamela and Hank grew up in a house. They had a backyard to play in. After the divorce I sold the house. I couldn't stand to live in it any more—the house where Cliff and I had had kids and had thrown a party a month. Cliff was a lawyer for a liquor company and got all the free booze he could carry home. God. Everyone loved to come to our parties. The bourbon flowed till four in the morning. I never drank it. Oh, maybe I would have one drink. But someone had to stay sober. My kids never saw me drunk. They can never say they did. I sold the house on impulse. It was after that when Hank moved away from me. He had been having trouble at Hyde Park High. A gang of boys were beating on him. I used that as the reason we moved, and in truth, it was, but it wasn't the only reason. I couldn't stand living in the house and trading at the same stores I had when I was married, and having people drop over who knew Cliff and me. I sold the house within months and moved across the city to the north side. I had no idea of the north side. I had lived on the near north side when I worked in the bookshop, and Claudia lived near north for years, but I had never ventured further north than Armitage. We rented a third floor apartment near Wrigley Field. I thought Hank would like that, but he hated it. He said he was a Sox fan. It's true, he was. He used to wait outside the Picadilly Hotel where the players stayed and get their autographs. The Picadilly was only three blocks from our house in Hyde

Park. We were crammed into this tiny apartment on the third floor. Pamela and I shared a bedroom. We each had a twin bed, and I used the ivory bedspreads that my mother had crocheted. Pamela said I snored too loud for her ever to get any sleep. Hank had his own room, but he hated it just the same. We lived off the house money, until I realized that it was going down the drain, and if I didn't get a house soon, we wouldn't ever have one. I didn't ask for alimony. Cliff can never say I bled him dry. I just wanted him to do right by the kids. God. No one can ever say I was money hungry like you hear some of those women are who take the men to the cleaners. By the time I found the house in Rogers Park, Hank was adamant: he was going to live with Cliff or run away. Cliff wasn't any too happy about it either. He was glad enough to pay the lousy $150 a month and only have to see the kids once a week. He was too busy with Delilah. God. How could I have been her friend? I didn't think they'd go for Hank living with them, but they sure surprised me. Oh, I could have fought it — the courts were on my side — I had full custody. And Cliff wouldn't have protested. But it was Hank. He began destroying things. He chopped holes in the bedroom wall of that apartment. God. Holes. Holes big enough to put a fist in. I think that's what he did. Just pounded on them till there were holes. I didn't know what else he would destroy before it was all over, so I let him go. It was a terrible day for me, the day he left. God. He packed all his things in cartons, and had a duffel bag from Boy Scouts. I had hired someone to patch all the holes by then. Cliff came and helped him carry down the boxes. What killed me was my own son wouldn't kiss me good-bye. He wouldn't even look in my direction the whole time he was moving things out. He just said, "See ya" when he left. Pamela didn't even get a mention. She was crying in our bedroom. She wanted to go too. That would have been the end of me. I told her to shut her mouth, that she wasn't going anywhere. What the hell was I buying the house for? Myself? God. A four bedroom house with just her and me here now. I've got the door to Hank's room shut. And I won't open it till he's back from Viet Nam in one piece. Not that he'll stay here much, but it's always there for him.

When Pamela came home that night, I told her that I lost my job and I didn't know what was going to become of us. She started crying, and she told me that she would go out and get a job, but I told her there were child labor laws. Then I called Claudia. Finally, after I told Pamela, I felt I could talk about it to someone. For once Claudia didn't open her mouth. She didn't have a thing to say. She just said she was sorry. I told her I didn't know what to do. That I felt everything was over. Nonsense, she said. There are other banks. But I told her I had been fired, well, not fired, because that would mean I had embezzled something, but "let go." How could I tell another employer that? She told me I would just have to, that I shouldn't mention it unless I was asked, but I had to try. "No one else can do it for you, Iris," she said. "Go tomorrow. Don't let any time go by or you'll be afraid to do it."

I got all gussied up—I even wore a girdle, which I'm not supposed to do because it restricts my breathing, and heels. I went to another bank in the neighborhood and walked in and asked for the personnel manager. He was a very nice man who patted my hand. I told him I could do a thousand checks a day, but I knew I could do better. Well, these weren't training grounds, he said. I told him I was accurate. I ended up getting the job because I had experience. My god. I had experience pounding a bookkeeping machine. I was so relieved that I got the job that Pamela and I celebrated by going out to dinner that night, to Ashkenaz Restaurant on Morse Avenue. Pamela ordered a Joey Bishop special and I ordered a Shelly Berman. They were both corned beef sandwiches with different things stuffed in them. I kept the new job for six months and was let go again. But I didn't feel as bad the second time. Because I had figured out that the bookkeeping departments were a round-robin kind of thing. By the time I left, JoAnn and Helen were both working with me and Opal was in another bank in the Loop. I finally ended up at the Freedom Commercial Bank six blocks away, and Helen and JoAnn were already working there the day I walked in. I've been there seven years and I've got my salary up to $525, which I know isn't much, but it's more than I was making when I first started with no experience. It looks like I won't lose this job because I can do two thousand checks easily now, and it's how many checks you can do that counts.

The thing about Pamela is she is so critical of me. The day I came home and told her I had hit the two thousand mark, she said, "Well, Helen can do three thousand, you said so yourself." I know Helen can do more than I can, but shouldn't she be happy for me? Two thousand is a lot. My god. I never thought my life would come to pounding on a machine. But it's the only thing I knew to do. Oh, I thought about going back to school after the divorce. But that costs money. The University of Chicago was affordable when Claudia and I went years ago. But one year's tuition, which is what I needed, would have broken my bank. God. I couldn't see going anywhere else. And there was no place to leave the kids. Claudia works all day. And she lived so far from us, it didn't seem possible for Pamela to travel there after school. Sometimes things just don't work out the way you planned for them in your life. I always thought I would have my degree, but it doesn't look like I will. But Pamela will, damn it. Why she can't see how hard I'm working for her, I'll never know. But later she'll appreciate all I've done for her. Her father certainly isn't any help. All Pamela does is nag me. Like with my ceramics. God knows, I want to work on my clay again. Does she think I spent years perfecting my technique only to let it wither away? God. Kids don't understand anything. I studied with Delilah, the best potter in the city, even though I hate to admit it. She taught me the coil method. My pots are as smooth as anyone's, and I don't have to use a potter's wheel to get them that way. As far as I'm concerned, a potter's wheel is like painting by numbers. Oh, I know a lot of people use the wheels, but it means so much more if you do it by hand. My god. My pots take forever, but they hold liquid, and people who've bought them say they last and last. I try to explain to Pamela, that I haven't given it up. All my equipment is in the little back room off the kitchen. I just haven't set up my kiln yet. I will. I'll have to get a 220 line put in and now those bastards want over $100 to do the wiring. When I had it done in Hyde Park it was $20. $20. I built the kiln myself, out of firebricks. And wired it myself. I didn't know how to do that, Delilah showed me how. God. We were such good friends. I trusted her, and all along I shouldn't have had her stay over at our house so much. She had her eyes on Cliff from the word go. She is a great potter. She had a firebrick kiln, and I was determined to have one just like hers. She told me where to order the bricks, and she helped me wire it, but I did most of it myself. Pamela was just a crawler then, and Hank was in kindergarten. I sat both of them on the kitchen floor and had them coil wire around a pencil. I used some of Hank's coils too. I let Pamela think that I used hers, but they weren't done right. But she tried. I built my kiln and kept it in our huge kitchen in back of the stove. I put thick asbestos pads around the walls. The kiln goes to over two thousand degrees. My god. That's a lot when you think of it. I was never so proud as the day I put my first naked vase in, powdery grey clay, and plugged in the kiln. The test cone melted, and I knew it was time to take it out. God. Of course I couldn't take it out right away, but when I finally lifted off the lid, there it was, all pink/beige and waiting to be glazed. It was a miracle, and I felt a surge of elation like I felt only two other times: when Hank was born and he was put in my arms when I woke up, and when Pamela was born and she was put in my arms and took my breast. I was too sick to nurse after Hank was born, so Pamela was my breast baby. I don't care what the modern people say about bottle babies being smarter, there was nothing better in the world than when Pamela took my breast. Nothing. To this day, Hank thinks I breast-fed him. I don't want him to think any other way, either. There's no reason he should have to know he's a bottle baby. He wouldn't take it right, I know he wouldn't, if he found out. Cliff is the only other person who knows and who might consider telling, but I know he won't. For all that's between us, I know he won't tell Hank that. Cliff really cared about me at that time. He was really worried that I wouldn't pull through. It was all because that bastard doctor wouldn't give me a Caesarean. He made me go through labor, knowing I had a weak heart from the rheumatic fever I had as a teenager.

All Pamela wants to know is when I'm going to start my clay again. I know what she's talking about. She wants me to finish the head. I started a bust of Hank when he was six. It was when we were in our other house. God. I propped him on a tall stool in the kitchen and he posed for me. It was a perfect likeness but I would never quite finish it. I would forget about it for a while. You can do that with clay. Just forget about it. You just put plastic over it. When you want to work on it again, you sponge it down until it gets pliable. So every few months I would work on the head, and then it got to be every year or so. God. When a year or two went by, I had to make major changes on it. I really saw Hank grow up making that head. I don't know why I haven't finished it. It sits out there to this day. Just five feet away from this kitchen table. I could open the door and see it now, shrouded in plastic. Hank at sixteen. That's the last time I worked on it. Now he's twenty, and I have a lot of catching up to do. Pamela nags me all the time to finish it. I tell her I can't finish it. I have to have the live model in front of me. Oh god. I can't keep the tears back when I think that. The live model. I do want to finish it. I want him to come back from that hellhole, that jungle, wherever he is — it's too far away, wherever it is, so I can finish that head. The worst part is not knowing where he is. That Special Forces he's in keeps his location secret at all times. God. I would give anything to have him sitting here next to me, even if he were cursing me out for making him sit here. I would give anything to finish the head, to make the leap from sixteen to twenty with a dab of the sponge and a scrape of the modeling tool.

Photo by Sandra Gregory

Take My Job, Please

Debra Riggin Waugh

Marcy, my supervisor, wants to meet with me at three o'clock. I don't know whether to worry or not. Then she says Jack, the big boss, wants to be there, too. I figure it's safe to worry.

On the way to the meeting, I ask Marcy what's up. It turns out that Jack found out that I said something to Carol, a friend of mine who works at our client's office, about my being pissed off about something Jennifer, a coworker, did. Well, Carol told Ron, and Ron said something to Jennifer, and Jennifer told Marcy or maybe even Jack, and he's pretty pissed — yep, pretty pissed.

So the three of us — Marcy, Jack, and I — meet in the conference room. Jack points out that this is a *serious* matter, and that he *seriously* considered letting me go. Sounds serious.

I think he's blown this thing way out of proportion, to say nothing of censorship, but I know better than to tell people who are overreacting that they're overreacting. I try to tell Jack that I understand why he's upset, but that I didn't see it as going over his head and talking to the client expecting results; I was just bitching to my friend (my friend who I used to work with, my friend who telephones me every morning to wake me up, my friend who takes care of my dog on those rare occasions when I go somewhere that doesn't allow dogs). My friend who happens to work at the client's office.

Then, Jack asks me why I'm unhappy at my job in general. Well, christ, where do I start. I'm unhappy because the company is unnecessarily cheap — low salaries and cheap equipment. I'm unhappy because I'm sharing an office that's only big enough for one person while Jack's office is big enough for three. I'm unhappy because I have to park at a parking garage down the street, and almost everybody else gets to park in our building. I'm unhappy because I have to sneak down to the alley and stand by a dumpster to smoke a cigarette.

But instead of saying all this, I start crying — *not* because I'm upset, but because I'm on the spot. Hell, maybe it's genetic. I don't cry often, but when I do, damned if I can stop. In between sobs, I even tell Jack and Marcy that I'm not that upset. Marcy leaves and brings me back Kleenex. Then Jack leaves and brings me back a Coke. All I really need is a cigarette. But they don't ask if I want to smoke, they just offer me Kleenex and Coke, so I take what I can get.

Jack points out that I'm up for my one-year salary review in a month. He wants to move it up to next week. I know what he's thinking: *Let's kick her while she's down.* I say that the only possible reason to move it up is to avoid giving me a raise. He disagrees. A few days later, Marcy tells me that she talked Jack into not moving up my review. I'm amazed because everybody knows men don't like to change their minds (also genetic). But he wants Marcy and me to rehash the whole thing in a week.

A week later, I walk into Marcy's office and sit down. She says you were late today. I say yes. She starts to say something else about me being late, and I say, I quit. She's flabbergasted. (The truth is I'm good and not so easily replaced.) Marcy says she hopes our meeting with Jack didn't precipitate this. I politely say it helped me make up my mind.

Two weeks later, I'm making $6,500 more a year, I'm smoking a cigarette with my feet up on my desk, and my new boss comes to work even later than I do. And I can tell Carol whatever I want. I win.

How Is This Week Different?

Ellen Gruber Garvey

New York City Transit Strike: Passover, 1980

Everyone is hoping to leave the office early: in a rush to get home for the Passover holiday, or just anticipating heavy traffic as the transit strike begins. The office manager paces along the rows of desks and whips around corners, checking to see that we're all still at our typewriters.

We'll never get done in time to leave early anyway; they've given us twice as many letters to type, though the office is out of white-out and carbon paper. And besides, we're in the middle of our break. We haven't even finished eating.

Behold the danish of our affliction, which our foremothers bought every morning at the coffee cart to solace themselves when they had been pulled too soon from their beds, their firstborn dreams taken from them and drowned in the second of the ritual four cups of coffee.

The office manager listens to the radio news, scratching his scalp. He's worried that we'll be marooned here by the transit strike, sleeping on the floor under our desks like wild animals. Then he'd be stuck here too, with the city dark all around and nothing to drink but the washroom's rusty red tap water.

The elevator brings corporate officers to our floor to drive us from our work stations. Management now doubts that the air-conditioning system will keep out locusts.

"Out," the office manager rasps. He has a frog in his throat. "Please leave now. We're closing up." We can't be sure whether to believe him. The decision is terrifying: If we go now, we may never be able to return. But if we delay, we may never be able to leave.

We approach the red-carpeted reception area. The strike starts. We are safe across. The office door shuts behind us.

But their hearts have been hardened. The office manager calls us at home from work. "How are you getting in?" he asks. "Can we put you in a car pool? Do you have a bicycle? When will you be in?"

We won't be. *With a mighty hand and an outstretched arm we are freed from the house of bondage. Horse and rider, rider and subway car, bus and railroad car have been thrown into the sea.*

Reasonable Facsimile
Bonnie Michael Pratt

The ghost of me walks these halls
shadowing in and out
of my fluorescent cube.
Elusive fingers reaching at me
leave only traces of my mind
to function here.
The work performs itself;
the words are spoken without me;
and even those who call me friend
do not know
that I was never here.

On Being a Secretary

Kathryn Eberly

I swear to god.
One day I went in to file
some papers and

suddenly realized the white plastic
astrological and kind of cosmic
(as in solar system) looking "thing"
on the shelf was actually an
IUD for cows.

It was then that it occurred to
me, a seminar on career options
might be appropriate.

Adjustments

Lesléa Newman

SHIFTING PILES

I place a pile of credits to my left
and a pile of debits to my right.
After I type the numbers from the debits
onto the credits
I pile the debits on top of the credits.
Then I pull the carbons from the credits
and separate the copies into piles.
I interfile the piles
and bring them over to the files
where I file the piles and pull the files
making a new file of piles.
Then I make files
for the pile that has no files
and put them into a new file pile.
I take the new file pile down the aisle
over to the table where Mabel
makes labels for April to staple.
I take the new labeled stapled file pile
back down the aisle over to the file
to be interfiled with the pile of filed files.
After I file April's piles
I get new debits from Debby
and new credits from Kerry.
I carry Kerry's credits and Debby's debits
back to my desk
and place a pile of credits to my left
and a pile of debits to my right.

After I type the numbers from the debits
onto the credits
it's 10:00
and we have exactly fifteen minutes
to go down to the cafeteria
and drink coffee
or go out into the parking lot
and scream.

COFFEE BREAK

Here comes the cake.
Will you look at that?
It's beautiful.
I don't know how he does it.
If you ever need a cake just ask Bob.
I had to carry it in for him you know
because of his wheelchair and all
you know and I had to hold it like this
because it was frozen you know
and God forbid I should fall.
Who brought in that cake yesterday?
The skinny one. You know, Alice.
Was that you Alice? You rat.
I can't help it. My landlord
gave it to me and I hate cake.
If I don't bring it in here it'll go bad
and I'll have to give it to my dog.
Listen to her. She gives it to her dog.
In my house it wouldn't last five minutes.
And she puts it right in front of me you know
I'm sitting there typing and I can smell the chocolate.
It's a good thing it wasn't mocha.
If it was mocha I would have slugged her.
I put the tea box in front of it and the coffee jar
so I wouldn't see it.
If it was mocha forget it. There goes my forty pounds.
You lost forty pounds! Really? How'd you do it?
Weight Watchers.
Really? Do you measure everything out and stuff?
No, not anymore. You get used to it. Your eye, you know.

I fill up on unlimited vegetables like mushrooms
and broccoli, you know? I can sit and eat a whole head
of lettuce in one night and not gain an ounce.
That's terrific.
You didn't try a piece did you Jackie?
Just a little piece.
Yeah right, a little piece seven layers thick.
Shame on you, a former Weight Watcher.
I know. I lost 25 pounds and put back 8 already.
But what'cha gonna do?
What a dreary day.
They say it's gonna rain all weekend.
It figures.
Hey Mabel, what's today's date?
The 23rd.
You know today I've been here for three years?
No kidding? It seems like you just started.
Time sure flies when you're having fun, right girls?
That's what I like about her, she's always joking.
You know who she reminds me of? Lucille Ball.
Yeah, you know you're right.
Someone said the same thing just the other day.
It's not the red hair and the deep voice so much,
it's the personality. She's always laughing.
Well you know what they say girls.
It's better than crying.

IVY

I worked here for two weeks
before I noticed the stem of ivy
that had crept in through a crack
in the wall and was growing slowly
across the carpet up towards
the African violet on my desk.
I pointed it out to April.
"Oh wow," she said.
"That should be on THAT'S INCREDIBLE
the TV show you know, where they have
all those interesting people on
doing all those interesting things
you know, like hanging upside down
out of an airplane or something.
You know, people do the most amazing things."

OUT TO LUNCH

We walk past the guard
on our way out to lunch.
"Let me see your ID," he says.
I unbutton my coat to show him
the badge he gave me four hours ago.
"*Oy vey*, do I ache," Debby says to me.
"Last night I went to an exercise class
and I can barely move."
"What kind of exercise was it?"
"Jazzercise."
"That's what you get for exercising
those old bones," the guard says.
"Now me, I say leave those old bones alone.
Hey girls, as long as you're going out for lunch
why don't you sign out now? Just put 5:00 right here.
That way you won't have to do it later.
I believe in making life easy."

PARANOIA

You know this afternoon I realized that
Kerry's hair isn't really blonde and
her makeup makes her eyes look a lot bluer
than they really are and I typed New Rock
instead of New York five times in a row
without realizing it and when Annie asked me
today's date I had to stop and think about it
for a really long time
and I didn't even see April standing right next to me
with a box of paper clips in her hand for five minutes
until she tapped me on the shoulder
and I can't even tell when the Muzak's on
or the Muzak's off anymore because of all the other noise
going on inside my head
and why do I always look up at the clock
at exactly ten minutes to four?
I have this funny feeling
that maybe Kerry was sent here from another planet
who's trying to take over the earth
so they cloned all these women to look like secretaries
and they're slowly dulling our minds
by making us type these numbers all day long
until our brains are about as useful as empty gas tanks
and I bet I could walk in here stark naked
or drop dead at my typewriter
and no one would even notice except maybe the janitor
who comes in once a week to empty the trash
and make the same joke, "Oh so your can's full again, huh?"

And maybe I've been reading too much science fiction
or smoking too much dope lately
but can it be only a coincidence that Kerry
just happens to be the first one in here every morning
making the coffee that the rest of us drink?
And oh shit I just typed $3,338.83
instead of $3,338.38 and you know Veronica
who sits behind Kerry
well she has dyed blond hair too
and come to think of it she mails in my time card
every week because she said it would be easier that way
but that means I have no record of my hours
so maybe this is all a dream
and I'm never really here
or maybe the rest of my life is a dream
and I'm really always here
and maybe it's too late and I'm the last one left
who hasn't been taken over yet
and they're waiting for me to surrender
so they can use this bank as their national headquarters
or maybe they have taken over the rest of the country
already and I should call the President
because I'm the only one left with any brains whatsoever
but I'm not even sure about that.

4:55

We shut off our typewriters
put our pencils into our pencil holders
screw the tops onto our jars of liquid paper
and glance at the clock
we place our unused envelopes
into our top left hand drawers
and our sheets of carbon paper
into our top right hand drawers
and glance at the clock
we lift our pocketbooks onto our laps
freshen our lipstick
pat our hair
and glance at the clock
we straighten our tangled rubber bands
check to see our typewriters are shut off
and glance at the clock
we inspect our fingernails
notice where the polish has chipped
and glance at the clock
we uncross our legs
and glance at the clock
we smooth our skirts
and glance at the clock

5:00

Bye
Goodbye
Goodnight
Have a nice night
You too
Take care
Have a good night
Good night
Good night

ODE TO THE SECRETARIES OF AMERICA

The Secretaries of America are spreading out
everywhere — with their orange silk roses
in thin white vases on their desks
next to pictures of their children or grandchildren
smiling at them through oval frames
next to jars of yellow and white liquid paper
lined up like nail polish
next to ceramic coffee mugs that say
WORLD'S GREATEST MOTHER or HAVE A NICE DAY
next to pencil holders made from orange juice cans
covered with construction paper
covered with glitter
with their sugar free chewing gum
tucked away in their pocketbooks
tucked away in their bottom left hand drawers
with their light blue cardigans
draped over the back of their swivel chairs
with their headphones on
listening to their bosses whispering
instructions into their ears
like some obscene phone caller —
O Secretaries of America
I hear you following me out into the parking lot
your high heels clicking on the pavement
your car keys dangling from your fingers
I see you walking through Waldbaums
with shopping lists in your hands
or waiting to buy whitefish at the deli counter

I hear you calling home on company time
to tell your teenage sons to take the roast beef out
and put it on low in the toaster oven
I see you at Elaine Powers Figure Salon
bending at the waist,
I hear you in diners munching on cottage cheese and carrot sticks
comparing the calorie content of pink and white grapefruit
I see you trying on skirts and slacks in Ohrbachs or Macys
looking over your shoulder at your behinds sighing in the mirror —
O Secretaries of America listen to me!
Take off your girdles and relax.
Stop wearing that lipstick —
it's made of pig fat, it's not even kosher!
And don't you know you don't have to make the coffee?
O Secretaries of America
get up off your chairs
and take a walk in the sun
or go home and smoke dope
with your teenage sons and daughters
and then pig out on carob brownies and M and M's.
O Secretaries of America
we love you just as you are
with your thick ankles and untweezed eyebrows
with your soft bellies and flabby thighs
we were born out of your bodies!
We nursed at your breasts or wanted to
we crawled into your lap
and let you rock us to sleep
we came to you crying with our scraped knees
and let you kiss it all better

O Secretaries of America
come crawl into my lap
tell me about your day
let me massage the back of your neck
your aching shoulders your tired feet
let me give you a good night kiss
before I tuck you in and shut the light.
O Secretaries of America
take tomorrow off
it's on me
take next week off
take next month off
O Secretaries of America
just take off

The Clerk's Lunch

Anya Achtenberg

The clerk will run blocks
to return a borrowed nickel
but she is always the last one
helped at the counter
where she can only afford
a cup of soup (split pea)
and a hard roll with a little butter,
which she tears apart,
one hill from the other,
not caring where the poppy seeds
fall, her hunger is so great.

Off Duty
Catherine Shaw

I won't go into detail.
That would be talking shop.
I will say only:
I have made many promises.
Some are set down in contracts;
others go unworded
but they bind me just the same —
in the breath, in the blood,
wherever ambition burns
or invention blossoms.
I am sworn.
I have made promises.
And when I have kept today's,
tomorrow's will want keeping
and next week's, next year's.
And even my dreams
are full of press and clutter
and when I wake from them
I wake late, and headachy,
and I have to get going,
I haven't a moment to spare.

All the same, a moment is what I did spare.
Just this morning, at the kitchen window,
I took a breath that nourished no ambition,
furthered no lofty need.
It met no deadline,
paid no outstanding bill.
It was time stolen, time won.
There was simply no accounting for it!

Certainly I had meant no pilferage.
I was simply drinking coffee —
a stoic's drink
and fuel for the engine too.
And my brain was fully occupied
with lists and schedules,
tasks of every kind.
But then I felt it:
the great hearth warmth.
Earth's own healer sun
was beaming in on me.
Clear through my sweater,
clear through my scrubbed skin
the heat bored.
And I wondered:
when had the season shifted?
How had the planet wheeled so near her star
without my taking note of it?
I touched my spoon:
The chrome was burning!
I closed my eyes:
the hubbub in my brain went mute.

My moment passed and I was out the door,
fluffing my hair
and thumbing my carfare nervously.
I had made a ten o'clock promise.
I was already five minutes late.

I'm Standing in Line

Rina Ferrarelli

I'm standing in line
for unemployment compensation
a long line that ropes around the room
waiting my turn
and hating it
because the clerk
who stands at the window hour after hour
or works at a desk squeezed between desks
in a mustard-colored room
with low ceilings and fluorescent lights
and no windows
the clerk makes it feel like a handout.

I go home and do laundry
and pick tomatoes for a salad
and when the children come home from school
late as usual and with long explanations
I sit and listen
and have a cup of tea while they have milk
and we talk about what they did today
and watch the cardinal
the one with the short flat crest
eat the stale bread in the driveway.

And next day I clean the fridge
and mop the kitchen floor
and when I get tired then or later
or fed up with housework
I sit by the window with a cup of tea
and watch the trees beginning to change
and the light with them
and tell myself that what you do
is not as important as how you live.
I could be that clerk
working in a mustard-colored box
making people feel like dirt.

Spotter
Candida Lawrence

I have been assured that "anyone can get a job at the Boardwalk," and I apply one blustery spring day. I am blown through the Personnel Office door wearing a skirt, black boots, a turtleneck, and a jacket. It is a weekday, and although the Boardwalk is closed, the Personnel Office is like a human hamster run. Attractive males rush down hallways, telephones ring, office girls smile and answer the switchboard, three applicants bend over their forms, chewing pencils.

I'm handed a form. There's a space for personal references which I fill with the same three names I always use: my former principal, Jack, and my friend Jane. I comb my hair while I await my interview.

The Personnel Manager smiles me into her office. She tells me she is a former first-grade teacher who much prefers the "breadth" and "liveliness" of her work at Surfside. She provides me with a history of Surfside's rise to corporate glory, its plans for expansion, and all the allied businesses. She announces that Surfside has more than nine hundred employees, most of them seasonal since the Boardwalk opens the week before Easter and closes after Labor Day.

"The employees are a varied and interesting group ranging in age from minors with work permits to senior citizens, and coming from an astounding variety of social and work backgrounds. Why last summer we even had a regent from the University working at the merry-go-round!"

She lists the various work areas: food services, cashiering, operating the larger rides (usually staffed by men). "There is one grandmother who has been an attendant at the merry-go-round for eight years. She just loves merry-go-rounds!"

I love merry-go-rounds too, but tend to cry as soon as I hear the music or see rapt children hanging onto docile mounts. Which area do I think I'd enjoy most, she wants to know.

"If I were to learn how to cashier, could I move from place to place?"

"Oh yes, we encourage our employees to learn all of the Park, and if you are not happy one place, you can try another. There's something for everyone."

"Cashiering then."

"Good. Oh, the pay is...do you know what the pay is?"

"I believe it's $3.35 an hour."

"Yes. And the shifts. We have day shift and night shift. Which do you think you'd prefer?"

"Day," I say, thinking of Jack and a lonely coyote-dog.

"Well fine, Alice, as soon as we check your references. Give us a few days and call my assistant. Oh, our employees are required to wear a uniform."

My first day at the Boardwalk is Training in Cashtronics, Tour of the Park, Orientation, and Wardrobe. Our cashier group meets at 12:30 in the office. Kate, our Supervisor-Trainer, is small with dark curly hair and thick glasses. She shrugs so much it seems almost an affliction; she clutches a clipboard to her chest. She gives off apology for her role and lets sentences die, uncompleted. The day is clear and sunny and since the Boardwalk is closed, our voices compete only with surf and sea gulls. I feel privileged being alive amongst so much disconnected, sleeping pleasure. How lovely the shape of the silent roller-coaster, the brightly painted booths, the clean walkways, the blunt-nosed kiddie-boats gently rocking in a circle of green water.

Kate unlocks the Ferris Wheel Ticket Booth and turns on the lights. The shades are down. Once the door is closed and locked behind us, we can forget ocean and sunshine. Kate seems to turn on a tape inside her mouth. She introduces us to cashbox, keys, ticket dispenser, knobs, buttons, reports, bracelets, strings and clips, Boardwalk Discount Clubs, voiding errors (especially important), organization of cash denominations, credit card box, counting change into customer's hand, where to put our purses, and how to save the customer money. She tells us all that the computer can and cannot do. She stresses what it can remember and how to make it forget.

There are three buttons you push to coax the computer into voiding an entry, which is what you must do when you make a mistake. "Just remember the buttons and the order in which I pushed them. Never, under any circumstances, forget to void tickets which have been sold and then the customer changes his mind, or you punch out too many, or whatever. The Boardwalk has Spotters, and you will never know when a Spotter is one of your customers. If the Spotter sees you not voiding, you may be fired."

Kate is impatient, and now seems to have no trouble finishing her sentences. I'm cold and want to see the ocean, want to be sure the door will open and let me out to the air and space. "Void" and "Spotter" flutter around in my head. I see the metal box opening its bowels, emptying the poisons of error into a vault under the ticket booth. I shiver with a sudden awareness of empty, indifferent darkness, our ticket booth dispatched into space, filling with 20-cent tickets, the button on the dispenser stuck, writhing yellow snakes. I must find the three buttons to void the contents before the Spotter...

"I don't expect you to understand it all today. Tomorrow you'll spend half the day watching a trained cashier and then she'll watch while you handle the window. Any questions?"

We smile uncertainly at Kate. She shrugs.

"OK, Alice. When you close, you do everything we did at the beginning, only in reverse. What is the first thing you must do to close?"

I stare at her. I can't remember anything we did, first or last.

"All right! Try to think! We've put a lot of stuff into the computer. We have to get it out and leave it empty. How are you going to do that?" She waits, tapping her pen on her clipboard. I touch three buttons lightly, afraid to push down.

"No no! That just voids the last entry. We have to get it all out. Don't you remember the first thing we did?"

"No, I don't."

"Watch!" She pushes three different buttons, the computer gurgles, then falls silent. "Now it has nothing in it. It has voided! Got that?"

I say yes, figure I'll get it later.

"Well, we can't spend any more time on it. We have to get to Orientation. Please watch me." She swiftly reverses her demonstrations, unthreads tickets, flicks switches, unhangs money bags, locks cash drawer, locks storage door. We watch.

"All right. What have I forgotten?"

We stare at her. The lights? Her manners? Tucking in the chairs?

"What did I use to turn on the computer? Is it just on all the time?" We stare at the mute thing with memory and bowels. Kate reaches down and pulls from its hole a tiny cube with prongs which I now remember her calling the "key," though it looks more like a flashcube. "I told you the key must be locked in the storage cabinet when you close."

Orientation is more fun. The Personnel Manager leads our "varied and interesting group ranging in age from minors to senior citizens" from one end of the Boardwalk to the final ride, a roller-coaster in a track of seawater. We see slides on the history of the Park and visit the underground workshop where bump cars are repaired and merry-go-round horses restored.

We stand under the big roller-coaster and look up through gears and tracks. Kate jokes with the three male supervisors. They seem to have a high regard and much affection for each other. It's a nice family, this Boardwalk group.

Coffee and cookies are provided in one of the ballrooms overlooking the ocean. While the others talk and joke, sip and bite, I stare out at the surf and think about Spotters. Isn't that what we called citizens during World War II who devoted part of their time to gazing at the sky, watching for planes coming in from the West? Civil Defense. And something my father used to say about Prohibition, about the danger of Spotters in speakeasies. Is it our very own American word? I dimly remembered the word used among girls in junior high school, when to bleed and be unprepared was the worst disaster we could imagine. Some of us were Spotters. Midway between the end of one Kotexed bleeding and the inevitable onset of the next, we "spotted." We never knew when it might happen, but we could feel a tiny cramp inside, hidden, and knew if we continued to sit, the spot might leak through for everyone to see.

"Is it the Curse?"

"No, I'm a Spotter."

"Geez, so's my sister. I'm sure glad I'm not . . ."

The leak of language. The flood of talk. A Spotter spots leaks. A Spotter leaks spots. Leak of juniper juice into dry mouths. Leak of enemy planes into peaceful skies. Leak of blood. Leak of cash. A corporation cramp, tiny but sharp, visible on cash flow tapes.

"Everyone will receive an Employee Manual. We'll take a few minutes now to go over what it contains. You, by your attitude, appearance, and conduct, will be our primary means of projecting the image of the Boardwalk. The most important thing for us to practice is almost too simple to believe: a smile! Your smile is your way of saying 'We are glad to have you with us'."

She smiles, teeth even, white, dazzling.

"Grooming Standards. There is more on that in the back of the Manual. Please be sure you read it. Beards are prohibited. You must be clean-shaven during all working hours. Neatly groomed mustaches are permitted. They must not extend past the corners of the mouth or below the upper lip. Braided corn rows and shaved heads are not allowed."

Pleasant laughter. I check my fellow employees. No corn rows, no shaved heads, several well-groomed mustaches, one beard. He looks startled. Will he leave? He hides behind his cup, sipping coffee.

"Evaluations. Your supervisor will review your performance and attitude, and will keep you posted. In the best of families misunderstandings and errors can occur. Discuss. With your supervisor."

Miss Kate, I think you're behaving like a bitch. Miss Alice, how can I be expected to train morons.

"Boardwalk Taboos. People look to us for the best in family entertainment. The following will be cause for disciplinary action, or dismissal: Indifference in performing duties, profane language, gambling or fighting, possessing or being under the influence of alcohol or drugs, insubordination, willful damage of company property, immoral or indecent conduct, falsification of company documents, fireworks or firearms, misappropriation of cash or tickets. If you believe in what you're doing, you will benefit from the great satisfaction that comes from having made a lot of people smile. Welcome to the Boardwalk! We are happy to have you with us! If you have not been issued a uniform, Wardrobe is open now. The supervisors and I will remain to answer questions."

I'm tired and want to go home to my dog and typewriter. My lips and teeth, even my ears are weary from smiling. Hoping to be first, I hurry to Wardrobe, but find an odd assortment of folk leaning against the walls, waiting to be measured, to try on, to sign for. The Wardrobe mistress is alone and frantic in her room of blue garments. 5:15. 5:30. 5:45. I do isometrics. I think about the uniform. There's a sign posted on the wall in front of me.

> The company-provided costumes which you will be wearing were selected by a committee composed of volunteers from each area. You may wear your costume to and from work, but do not wear it at any other time.
>
> The women's tops must be zipped all the way up. No shorts. If you wear a sweater or shirt under your top, it must have short sleeves. No apparel is to be seen other than your uniform.
>
> Shoes must be closed-toe variety. No thongs, sandals, or clogs permitted.
>
> Baubles, bangles, and beads are too much. Women's earrings must be of the post or small lobe type. Only one earring per ear. Men may not wear earrings.
>
> Sunglasses must not be mirror type. You must wear your name tag at all times.
>
> SMOKING will be permitted as long as it is done in good taste. NO SMOKING IS PERMITTED WHILE YOU ARE INTERFACING WITH A GUEST!

142

I watch people change from clothes of their own choice to a costume "selected by volunteers from each area." The young almost carry it off, but the older ones, especially the women, seem injured, their bodies reluctant and diminished. Suddenly I love my cotton turtlenecks, my blue jeans and open-toed sandals. How can I bear to wear that top. I hate the blue in the panels and piping and collar, the blue you see on boxes of Cheer, magic marker blue, kindergarten blue, sign blue, junior-high blue bloomers with hurting elastic around the thighs. I try to think of flowers that color. Pansies are darker, bachelor's buttons lighter, vincas...no, no. Every blue I can think of in nature or art has more white, more grey, more yellow, more red. The tops are two-tone and the second blue is light. That's its name, light blue. Does the other blue have a name? The pants are navy blue.

I am measured and given two tops and two pair of pants to try on. It's cold in the changing room and I'll be damned if I'll take off my turtleneck. The pants don't fit, the 10 too large, the 8 too small. Both are too short. The Medium top is too large all over. If I don't zip the Small and turn up the sleeves an inch, I can still move my arms. I try not to look at myself in the full-length mirror.

I keep the small top and return all the rest. She gives me pants with elasticized waistbands. My uniform sits on the car seat beside me. I want to sling it into a mud puddle and stomp on it. I'm in a foul mood.

The next morning my dog looks at me in my uniform with nonregulation long-sleeved T-shirt under the two-tone top (unzipped so I can lift an arm to comb my hair). She lowers her soft grey ears and slinks outside to hide under the bamboo. She doesn't whine to go with me. She's not sure she knows me.

I punch my first time clock at 11:30 a.m. Kate (not in costume) introduces me to my trainer.

"Good morning, Alice. This is Mary. She'll work with you and reteach you what we rushed through yesterday. By twelve o'clock you should be able to take over the window. Mary will watch and answer questions. Zip up, Alice, and remove your T-shirt."

Mary seems pleasant enough but she mumbles and stoops to pick up bits of paper as we stroll to the Ferris Wheel Booth. Inside the booth, she sets down her cashbox and says: "You can open up."

"I'm afraid I can't remember what to do first." I pretend my ignorance disconcerts me. It's ten minutes to eleven and although we can't see through the closed slotted shades, we know the customers are already lined up outside. Mary doesn't hurry. She changes her shoes and complains that her feet are swollen. At ten minutes after eleven, after we have gone through the opening procedures helter-skelter, Mary hands me a plastic bag filled with orange metal clips. I'm to stack them in piles of ten. I like this lazy learning.

Kate, eyes wild, is suddenly standing between us. "Mary! Open that window! Never mind the clips!"

"She's countin' 'em."

"Fuck it, Mary! I said forget the clip-counting and get your window open!" Her pager is beeping. The telephone is ringing. I'm paralyzed. Kate departs to open the slats, and there it is, "the whole world passing by."

During the next hour I watch Mary's performance. Simultaneously, she counts cash, jabbers with customers, pushes buttons, absorbs tickets. The trickiest part is the right hand whose third and fourth fingers neatly collect tickets which burp from a slot, while her thumb wanders off to punch more buttons. The transactions seem to melt into each other without beginning or end.

At 12:15 Mary offers me the window. She lights up a Pall Mall. My first problem is the maneuver with the burping tickets. My fingers get ready but the yellow tickets, instead of piling correctly into my grasp, flower riotously like time-lapse marguerites, blossoming out of control, and I have to stop to collect them with both hands. And I seem to have a wandering right elbow which hits the dispenser button, the one marked $8 that issues twenty tickets in rapid succession.

"You'll get it, just keep tryin'," Mary soothes.

"This...mess...I think I'm supposed to void them. Right?"

"Oh hell, just put 'em to one side and we'll sell 'em to another customer and won't punch it. Much easier that way."

144

"But . . ."

"Kate don't like it and I know it's not company policy, but hell, it's so much easier."

At one o'clock Mary tells me to take a fifteen-minute break. I know what time it is because I stare at the clock to make sure it's functioning. It feels like four o'clock.

Outside, I want to walk on the beach but my uniform is so tight and beach walking is so loose that I wander instead down the Boardwalk to the merry-go-round. As soon as I hear the music I start crying.

Certain I am late, I run back to the booth. I look at the clock. Five minutes early. It must be running backwards. For the next two hours I practice the hand trick with no noticeable improvement. And I get lots of experience in not voiding. It's a good system.

On my second fifteen-minute break, at four o'clock, I have a problem to present to Kate. I find her in her underground office.

"How goes it, Alice?"

"Well . . . fine. I'm learning. But I have a problem. It's very hard for me to work in a small room with people smoking. Is there some other place I could be?"

"I sympathize with you. I feel the same way. In fact, I haven't seen my mother for two years because I won't let her smoke in my house or car, and she feels I just don't like her. However, I have trouble enough scheduling work combinations and if I had to figure out who can't work with smoke, etc., etc., it would be too much."

"Still, could you . . ."

Mary walks in. I look at Kate. I feel sure she'll change the subject.

"So eventually, maybe we can find a station where you won't have to be bothered by smoke, but for the time being, you'll just have to bear it. Hi Mary! Who's relieving?"

I feel a cramp deep inside me, a signal of blood. When we're back in our booth, Mary says, "Why din't you tell me my smoke bothers you? I can smoke outside or in the corner. You shouldna told Kate."

"I thought she could move me. You were here first." I'm not saying what I mean. I feel like a company fink. A Spotter.

At 5:15 Kate tells me I may go home and Mary will close. I punch out but for some reason the check-out time prints on top of the check-in time. I'm too tired to correct it.

I sleep nine hours.

Sunday morning I want to stay home. When I put on my costume, my dog hides again under the bamboo. I check in and Kate gives me my cashbox. I walk through the crowds to the ticket booth where Mary waits for me. She lets me open up and all goes well. The customers are nice, my right hand has learned how to gather tickets. The clock is still not working properly but I've adjusted.

The trouble begins around noon. A man is at the window and I count out change for a $5 bill. The bill sits to my left. I'm always careful not to put the money in the cashbox until the customer walks away.

"I gave you a ten. Where's my change?" he says.

"I believe you gave me a five. It's right here."

"I gave you a ten. Gimme my change."

"No, here's your five. Right here."

He turns to the man standing beside him. "I gave her a ten and she's trying to cheat me. Didn't I give her a ten? I remember what was in my wallet. Remember we didn't know if we had enough cash to come here. It was a ten, wasn't it?"

Spotter? Customer? I look over at Mary. She speaks through the window at him. "Mister! Hold your steam! We'll call the supervisor. Step to one side, please."

"GODDAMMIT! Gimme my change! Damn are you STUPID!"

Mary is talking on the phone and I'm sitting here doubting. If he's so sure, maybe he's right. I'm not positive. That five could have been sitting in that spot all morning. Kate slams through the door, her pager beeping. "OK, what happened?"

"I think he gave me a five. He thinks he gave me a ten. Here's the five, but..."

"STUPID DAME! GIMME MY CHANGE! FUCKIN' CROOK!"

Kate steps outside. He must leave his name. Company rules. He will receive his money by mail if he is right. She returns.

"Mary, take the window. I want to talk with Alice. OK, these things

146

happen. Now he's mad and he's going home. He's given me his tickets and I gave him a five. We want to void the tickets. What must we do?"

"I...I can't remember."

"Alice! I told you yesterday how to void! Are you telling me you didn't make any mistakes yesterday? Didn't you void all day?"

"Yes...no...I made mistakes."

"So, you made mistakes. What did you do about it?"

"I...we...we used another system."

"What system?"

"We put the tickets to one side." Cramp in my gut. I bend over to ease the pain.

"Mary! Goddammit! You know how to void, you know what you're supposed to do!"

"Yeah Kate, calm down. I'm sorry."

"Alice, that man could have been a Spotter, and I'm telling you right now, if you use Mary's system again, you'll be subject to disciplinary action. Everything you do in this room has to go into Cashtronic memory. Do you understand?"

"Yes."

"Take fifteen. I'll be back later to observe."

For fifteen minutes I lean against a garbage can and think about finking twice in forty-eight hours. I know I have to go back to Mary and say something, but what? I hurt and can't stand up straight. I wonder if my dog is still under the bamboo and what would happen if I quit right now. Happen to me, that is, to the pain.

I put my hand on Mary's shoulder and squeeze. It's all I can think to do.

"You shouldna told Kate about not voiding."

"I know, but I either had to say something or quit. I shouldn't have said I had made mistakes, but she wouldn't have believed I hadn't. I don't feel pleased with myself."

"Oh forget it. Just watch out for her. Here, take the window."

The clock stops altogether and Mary goes outside to smoke. Kate comes in to observe, silently, and while she is there, pain stabs, my hands tremble, tickets blossom again, the customers fuss, and I can't hear. I have to ask each mouth to repeat and put my ear against the window. Seven hours with two fifteen-minute breaks. I ask Mary to call Kate and tell her I'm tired and want to go home. A sweet girl named Becky (Head Cashier) arrives.

"OK, now you can close."

She gently leads me through the counting of cash, unplugging, reports, clearing the memory, wrapping what's left over.

"I was up at four this morning cleaning bars with my husband. I'm not tired," Mary says.

6:00 p.m.

"Kate wants to see you before you leave. In her office," Becky says gently.

Kate offers me a seat, but I prefer to stand, pleading buttock fatigue. "What are your feelings about the job? Is there anything you'd like to discuss? I have the sense that you are somewhat unfocussed and I wonder about the cause. Can you express it? Smoke-in-the-booth? Customers-coming-too-fast? Noise-in-the-booth? Something else?"

She's looking at me through her thick lenses. Her clipboard is ready, her pencil poised.

"Perhaps it's the Kate-suddenly-in-the-booth-to-observe which unfocusses me. I don't have all that much trouble when you're not there."

"Touché! I like you, Alice. And I want you to succeed."

She talks, I listen. She seems to be trying to grill me about Easter week, to pin me to a promise I didn't make. What did the Personnel Manager say to me? And then what did I say? The pain. I wish I could put down my ears, crawl under the bamboo.

I punch the time clock at 6:30. Again punch-out humps punch-in. Six-thirty is closing time for the Boardwalk and it takes half an hour to go two blocks. My dog cheers up when I take off my costume. I fold it neatly, placing ID card and name tag on top. She sniffs the pile. Tomorrow, or next week, sometime, I'll return what belongs to them. Or maybe I can hire someone to do it.

148

High and Low
Holly Hildebrand

She never complained of the indignity,
the way, still crouched on the floor,
she had to gather up the boxes,
listen to the mocking of the tissue paper
rattling beneath her fingertips,
face the last whiff of the rebels
whose owners had rejected her, saying things like,
"They pinch," or "My toe rubs at the front,"
or, worst of all, because she never knew why,
"No, I don't think they're right."
Sometimes, remembering the state of their nails,
or noticing that their socks hadn't matched,
or that they had, out of vanity,
worn a size too small for too long,
she would feel superior, vindicated,
when they walked away, their feet
carrying the same weight as before,
because their wallets were no lighter,
and their hearts had not been touched.
In these moments, she would remember her own feet,
tiny like those of a Japanese princess,
so slender she needed the elusive Slim,
and she would bury her hatred of them
in the shoe boxes, like coffins,
that lined the shelves of her sanctum,
the place where they were never allowed,
the room where she would disappear,
keeping them in her power for a few minutes,
checking on whether she had it,

the sequined pump, the black spike heel,
the Italian loafer, the ruby-red slippers
that would work their charms, cast their spells,
whisk them from lowly earth to the highest clouds,
if only she could produce it, in 8 1/2 AAA.
Sometimes, she would keep them in suspense,
pretending she had overlooked it, bringing out
boxes of others, unsuitable to their dreams:
navy-blue walking shoes, heavy-soled wing tips,
solid Oxfords when they asked for pastel sandals.
Sometimes she even convinced them that these were what
they wanted — she dropped words like *cushioned impact*
and *fallen arches* — and they nodded, worried,
frowning a bit as they agreed to take them.
But these were the ones she despised the most,
they were too easy, pushovers in their fallen nylons,
and when she retired, after thirty-eight years,
she spent most of her time barefoot in her garden,
all the shoe boxes in her house dusty except one,
which contained the only thing she had ever wanted:
cerise patent leathers with satin bows,
still one size too large for their owner.

The Circle of Chairs

Bernice Rendrick

For my aunt, Clara Majors

In her dry-goods store a haphazard
collection of chairs circled
the coal stove: peeling wicker
from the sun parlor, a blurred
needlepoint beyond its prime,
an oak rocker with a broken arm
and a kitchen pine of many Joseph coats
that served faithfully six days a week.

Miss Clara climbed the ladder, her thin
arms pulling muslin and gingham
from rainbow shelves. As women rocked
and gossiped, flannel thumped
across the counter, and tatting shuttles
flew like tongues. Apron patterns were
traced on tissue, while wool, harsh
as a scratchy throat, was folded
into brown bags. Daisy chains were looped
and linked, bluebirds opened wings
on baby bibs. In spring, satin whispered
across the measuring plank and from
the island of linens a bride's gift
of sunbonnet pillowcases was chosen.

A recipe for jonquil cake traveled
the circle as buffalo nickels roamed
from the cash register to children's
pockets, quarters turned up in
birthday hems, until the chairs
emptied, and Miss Clara leaned the
CLOSED sign against the pale mannequin.
Hunched over her books at the desk
she tried to balance, always
came up short. Pushing worrisome
wisps of grey hair into the net
she'd order more yardage and thread
knowing they'd soon need Easter clothes.

152

Photo by Marianne Gontarz

Huevos
Diane Lefer

La Estrella de Oro — The Gold Star — started out as a simple and decent stationery store. Doña María stocked paper, pencils, rulers, a few books on religious and occult themes and biographies of John F. Kennedy, the good Catholic who was certain to change things up North. She took orders for personalized Christmas cards. The proceeds were scanty, but at least her children would get their school supplies at wholesale price. Doña María also lent out small sums from the money her late husband had left her. She lived above the store with four daughters and with Consuelo, the maid. Doña María could have easily managed the house and kitchen — especially with four daughters to help her — but if she didn't have a maid, customers would not take her very seriously as a businesswoman. For the same reason, Luz was hired to assist in the store.

La Estrella de Oro had been the simple shop of a decent widow when Luz accepted the job. She was thirteen years old and lived with her aunt, uncle, and cousins in San Tomás el Grande. In other words, she was a country girl. Luz walked to the railway signal stop each day before dawn for a twenty-minute ride to the nearest town where she could get a bus connection to the city.

From the bus terminal she walked another mile to the store. If it was raining very hard and she had an extra twenty centavos, she sometimes took a city bus from the terminal, but that meant she might not have the money to take the bus at night when she was tired, and she hated to walk through the dark streets alone.

The pay was low, but Luz was satisfied enough with her job until Doña María began to expand her horizons. She invested in an ice chest, which stood at the front of the store. Early each morning, sometimes even before the metal door had been rolled up to open the store onto the street and even before Luz had swept and mopped the sidewalk clean, the iceman would arrive.

154

While Doña María had him load the chest and paid him, Luz would hurry up the back stairs to the storeroom for a selection of sodas. After a month they began to place orders with the ice cream vendor as well.

Luz had no objections to expanding business. The increase in her duties was negligible, and if Doña María cleared more money, there was always the possibility of a raise. The problem was that the ice-cold Coca Colas began to attract a different kind of client. Before, an occasional quiet student came in for a notebook, or maybe the day started with a tourist looking for a few envelopes and stamps. Now *La Estrella de Oro* became a hangout for young, teenaged boys.

Doña María was not concerned. These were boys from nice families. Ruffians had better things to do than drink Coca Cola and flirt harmlessly with shopgirls. Doña María had been a teenager once herself, but for some reason she had quite forgotten that to a sensitive thirteen-year-old girl like Luz, teasing attentions of members of the opposite sex are hardly harmless.

The most shameless was a skinny boy with glasses. Luz could sneer to herself when she was alone—the boy had an obvious need to prove his manhood; he was pathetically insecure. But when he came in and swaggered up to the counter, saying, "Nothing like a cold drink when you're hot," in a dirty kind of voice so that the rest of the group giggled, Luz reddened with shame. People would suspect there was something funny or bad about her if boys like this felt entitled to talk to her that way. She didn't like to hear boys giggle. That was for girls and women. Men were supposed to laugh out loud. There was something ugly about a male giggle.

But the ice chest was only the start. Doña María was pleased with her increased receipts and decided to go into the egg business.

Luz could never understand how a decent widow could have made such a decision. Doña María didn't even tell her in advance, but as soon as the egg man arrived one morning and Luz was instructed to set up a display in the center of the store, she knew exactly what to expect.

Doña María must have known. After all, she had been a married woman. She had given birth to four children. Surely she knew more about such things than Luz did. Luz set to making the little sign that

Doña María requested: "Huevos—40 centavos." Her hands shook. *Huevos* meant "eggs," but surely Doña María had to know it also meant "testicles."

Luz stationed herself behind the counter and fixed her eyes on the floor. It would be a hard day.

The boys were delighted.

The skinny one pranced up to her. In a most refined tone of voice, punctuated by snickering from his friends, he tried first to establish eye contact with poor Luz. "Excuse me, Miss," he said, "do you have *huevos*?"

Luz had spent the morning anticipating the question and trying to come up with an answer. If she said yes, she had fallen into the obvious trap. If she said no, the boy would pretend he was talking all along about the kind of *huevos* that were on display in the center of the store. It would be clear that Luz—not he—had a filthy mind, and that she was preoccupied with subjects of which a decent girl would have been totally ignorant. If she pointed to the display, she would be answered with a leer. "Those don't look like *huevos* to me," he would say.

"You can see for yourself," would have been a clear invitation to disaster.

"Leave me alone!" would lose her the job.

"Take two—you need them," was the most tempting response, but the one that was most impossible for a country girl like Luz.

It was a perfect question. A perfect trap. Luz stood frozen.

"Excuse me, Miss," he repeated. "Do you have *huevos*?"

Luz didn't know much about dealing with boys but she knew a lot about salesmanship. In that moment, to her good fortune, her salesmanship took over and the answer poured naturally from her lips. "Fine hens' eggs we have, indeed," she replied, "delivered farm-fresh this morning. At forty centavos each, very cheap."

The boys hooted at their friend. For a moment, Luz had won their respect.

But the skinny boy would not be outdone. He put eighty centavos on the counter and went to pick up two eggs. He returned and stood in front of her, smiling, balancing one egg in each of his cupped hands and moving his fingers. She knew very well what the gesture meant. It was an obscenity she accepted easily when her uncle made it, cupping his hands when he talked sarcastically of some big shot with a lot of nerve. She'd heard lots of dirty words from her uncle and learned all the gestures, but he could drink and swear without embarrassing her. He laughed out loud. He wasn't like these self-conscious boys with changing voices who focused their eyes on her chest and talked about *huevos* and giggled.

The boys played catch with the eggs until a shy one with long lashes kept one and began to pantomime. He strutted around like a woman. He played at opening a cashbox and making change. He made it very clear that Luz was the model for his act.

Luz wouldn't look. She counted the money in the cash drawer again and again. The boy stroked the smooth white shell; then he punctured it at the bottom with a penknife. His mouth covered the hole and he sucked out the egg, rolling his eyes.

His friends whooped. "Go to it!" they shouted. The shy boy never said much, but could he ever act!

Why did Doña María leave her down here alone?

What would people think of her?

Luz cried all the way home.

La Estrella de Oro was located on Calle Independencia — Independence Street. It was a fine location. It was only two blocks from the open market, so many people passed that way. But it was a store, a real store, and not merely a market stall. The store owners and employees along Independencia were very proud of the distinction, yet in ways they would not admit they would have liked to be in the marketplace themselves. There the women who sat amid their wares weren't separated from one another by solid walls. They shared their food and gossiped and minded one another's children.

The people on Calle Independencia were too professional for that.

All up and down the street shopgirls stood in the doorways, reciting the bargains of the day and inviting passersby to enter. And by standing that way, half in the street, they could look up and down and see all the other shopgirls. People passed, and some stopped in a store and some didn't. The patter of the shopgirls made little difference to the potential customers, but these advertising duties were important to the girls. They had an excuse to stand in the doorways and gossip and inspect one another's clothes just as their less professional counterparts could do more easily a couple of blocks away.

Luz stayed in the back of the store or behind the cashbox these days. She began to get the reputation of a snob.

"Doña María," people would warn, "your girl is too lazy. She doesn't do a thing to attract customers. She's always in the back. She's bad for your business."

Doña María shrugged. "Business is good," she answered. There were so many boys hanging around. They bought all their school supplies from her now and the sale of sodas was brisk. They even bought eggs, strangely enough. Surely things had not come to such a state in the middle class that mothers sent their sons out to do marketing!

In the back of the store Luz dreamed of escape. She couldn't get another job on Calle Independencia, not with the reputation she had. She'd heard of girls working as maids in Los Angeles. The money was good and the work easy. All you did was push buttons, she'd heard—the actual work was done by machine. Luz wondered how you could get a job like that, how you could cross the border. Los Angeles was probably out of reach. If she saved her money, maybe she could take the bus to Mexico City or Guadalajara, but her mother had once warned her about what could happen to a girl alone in the big city.

Luz longed for a safe way out. At seventeen she considered marriage the obvious step. But on Independencia, Luz had no friends, and in San Tomás all the boys had gone away to look for work. So what was an ordinary person like Luz supposed to do? It was probably better not to think about things like that.

"You'd better keep an eye on that girl of yours," people told Doña María, "with all those fellows she's got hanging around." And why were they hanging around? Doña María looked Luz over carefully. She was still a skinny child, still flat on top. Since the dentist had yanked two of her molars her cheeks sagged, and even her pretty face had lost its charm. Doña María knew that sometimes unattractive girls were the first to take the most fateful steps. They felt they had to. But when did Luz have the time? Well, no matter how she attracted the boys. The boys knew how to spend.

During the windy season Doña María liked to stay in bed late with the quilt pulled up around her. Luz would have to see to the iceman and the egg man herself. She would inspect the delivery carefully. A certain amount of breakage was expected and the egg man knew just how much he could get away with. At a quarter of seven Consuelo would go downstairs for the cracked or broken eggs which would serve for the morning's breakfast.

After breakfast the children stopped by and said good morning to Luz on their way to school. In the afternoons after school the girls played soccer in the storeroom. Luz had never much liked Doña María's precious offspring—they were spoiled and lazy, every one. When the soccer games began, Luz resented them even more, because this gave her something new to worry about.

The storeroom was a long passageway, built like an interior balcony over the store. If a customer was looking for a special notebook, or paper of a certain color, and had trouble describing it, Luz could ring for Doña María. She or Consuelo would come downstairs and guard the cashbox while Luz ran up to the storeroom. There she would hold up samples to the customer until a suitable item had been found. It saved the bother of carting a large assortment up and down the stairs until the customer was satisfied. Most important, as soon as the customer said, "Yes, that's it," Luz could toss the article over the rail to Doña María. The sale would be completed even before Luz could rush down the stairs and back to her post. The speed and efficiency with which a customer could buy an unusual item kept only in the storeroom was a matter of pride to Doña María. "That's the kind of service people have a right to expect on Independencia," she would say.

Thus the interior balcony was a perfect storage space. Luz, however, did not think it was a perfect soccer field. Any wild kick was quite capable of making the ball jump the rail and land in the store. Luz had been hit in the head once. Another time a pile of notebooks was knocked right off the shelf. And when the ball bounced out into the street, of course Luz had to run after it and toss it back to the screaming children. All this had been a nuisance, but a tolerable one. Now with the eggs to worry about, Luz stiffened all afternoon in time to the *thwack-thwack* of the ball rebounding from the ceiling and walls. Once she had run out from behind the counter and caught the ball just before it would have landed squarely on the gleaming white pyramid of fragile shells. No one thanked her or congratulated her for her quick reaction. Obviously, then, protecting the eggs was part of the responsibility that fell within the province of the shopgirl. To Luz that meant that if the children ever did succeed with a direct hit, the cost—by now sixty centavos apiece—would be deducted from the shopgirl's wages.

One more burden to be borne. In spite of her growing resentment, Luz felt a concerned affection for the four little girls. They would pay a price for their fun in the end. She worried about them. When they grew up, what would it mean to them to have to live above an egg store? ("Does your mother have *huevos*?") There was no limit to wickedness. Doña María's daughters were born to suffer.

In the early '70s, Mexico led the Third World. It was safe to talk about Cuba again. Doña María stopped ordering religious books and began to stock Cuban literature. For a while the store sold Che Guevara T-shirts, too, and offered local soft drinks instead of Coke.

Luz listened to the students discussing revolution and reading aloud from the newly acceptable books.

Fidel and his men had trained for a while somewhere in the state of Veracruz. Mexico, then, had a firsthand involvement in the historic events in the Caribbean. The revolutionaries hadn't been afraid of death. Prison had held no terrors. Luz heard the story of Haydée Santamaría, one of the valiant women who had fought to save Havana from being the Yankees' weekend brothel. While imprisoned by Batista, she was awakened one morning for breakfast. "Would you like some *huevos*?" said the jailer with a smile. He lifted the cover from the breakfast platter and showed Haydée the testicles of her lover.

One Sunday shortly after church, a new blue Volkswagen covered

160

with fresh dust from the dirt roads pulled up in front of the wooden shack where Luz lived in San Tomás el Grande. The car was followed by some curious children who had sighted it at the railway crossing. The children felt they'd played an important role in the drama. They had told the driver where he could find Luz.

Felipe López got out.

Luz saw him from the window. Though filled with horror, she had the presence of mind to give her little cousin a peso and send him down the road to bring back a bottle of Coke.

Of all her tormentors, Luz hated Felipe López the most.

Felipe was the son of the family that owned the hardware store at the corner of Independencia. He worked there behind the counter when it suited him. Most of the day he strolled. And several times a day it suited him to stroll past *La Estrella de Oro*. Several times a day he would buy an egg, making the obscene cupping gesture with his hand. Then, in plain view out on the sidewalk, he would toss the egg in the air and let it spatter on the concrete.

Now, Luz knew full well that very few of the young men bought eggs because they really needed or wanted them. But Felipe was the only one who didn't eat what he bought. Luz had gone hungry at times in her life. Felipe's ostentatious display of wealth disgusted her. There were people whose lives could have been transformed by the several pesos he let break on the sidewalk and dribble down into the gutter every day.

"Don't you ever get bored with this?" she asked him once, angrily.

"Yes," he had answered.

Felipe was rich and attractive. If it hadn't been for the eggs, Luz could have admired him from a distance. She would never have known the truth about his ugly personality. Of course, she thought, without the eggs he never would have paid any attention to her, but that would have been better. She could have sighed over an impossible love. She would have been invisible to him forever. But under the circumstances, he had to think of her as cheap, and she was only too aware of his imperfections.

Her aunt, uncle, and cousins crowded around with smiling faces and watched Felipe drink the Coke. How had little Luz managed to hook a man like this one? After all, Luz was twenty-six already. You stop thinking of an unmarried girl as a female at that age. You start to treat her differently. How, then, had Luz managed to lure this young man out into the barren countryside?

Perhaps it was just curiosity; perhaps he was just slumming. Still, idle curiosity can easily be turned into another kind of interest, reasoned the aunt. Whatever the fellow's motives, he was a good catch and he was seated in the patio. It was the chance of a lifetime.

Only Luz sat silent and sullen, her humiliation masked in cold disdain. When circumstances make you look cheap, she realized, you have to be ever on guard to ward off easy assumptions. Luz was not as naive as her family. She was sure that Felipe was only making fun of her. Luz had given up hoping for love. Now she stared at him, demanding respect.

Luz couldn't relax any more; she learned to be severe.

The government changed hands every six years and sometimes shifted its philosophy radically. *La Estrella de Oro* kept in step but never regained its former glory. Business was slack.

When the conservative government came in, *La Estrella de Oro* became a quiet place to work. There were no more lively debates. The rulers were imprinted with the Golden Rule; Doña María disposed of the remnants of the leftist days with their telltale slogan: "A line as straight as the People's March to Justice." She started a bookshelf devoted to the subject of Unidentified Flying Objects and another shelf to books on reincarnation.

Luz wasn't a teenager any more. The boys had grown up and looked for more grown-up pastimes. The new little boys found new little shopgirls to tease.

Doña María's daughters had babies now. Luz was shocked, but Doña María took the mishaps in stride.

"I could send them to the United States, where these things don't matter," she said. "They'd be able to get married there. But the way most men are, they won't miss anything, not having husbands."

So the daughters stayed home. Luz didn't dream about the United States anymore either. She was thirty; she was old; she had one life and one job and that was that. What was the point of running away? She had left home once to seek her fortune. She'd put on shoes and come to town to work in a shop, and it had been a mistake.

"Of course, my late husband was the exception, a saint," said Doña María, "but still, I was happy enough God took him when He did. He gave me my babies, and that's all I ever wanted of that man."

Grandchildren played soccer in the storeroom. The little boys were as healthy and attractive as their mothers.

Up and down Independencia, people talked about the downfall of Doña María's girls. Luz resisted efforts to draw her into gossip about the family. Privately she had her opinion: when you shower a girl with trinkets all her life, it's no surprise that she's quick to take a little gift under the skirts.

Luz stood in the doorway now and called to passersby to enter. No one tried to get fresh. People on Independencia still thought she was a snob.

Luz wondered what her aunt would have said if she, Luz, had ever come home with a baby.

Mornings, after washing the sidewalk clean and filling the ice chest, Luz went to work on the egg display. People didn't have much money these days. *La Estrella de Oro* had begun to stock brown eggs as well as white, offering the broken ones at bargain rates. Luz stacked the pyramid carefully, with an eye to art and practicality. She liked to create fields of color and also to be sure that any number of eggs of either type could easily be picked without disturbing the balance and causing a slide.

Women came in with plastic shopping bags, and young girls running errands. The women were invariably polite and the servant girls had sweet, fresh faces. To them, an egg was an egg.

Luz rang up the purchases. The eggs were clean and shiny and innocent. They were nutritious and cheap. Who could have guessed that this simple job and these graceful, fragile shells could turn a life from its expected course?

Luz never walked from the bus any more. She was too tired.

In San Tomás el Grande, Luz had taken to telling stories. Before she had come to live with her relations, she said, she had been at a plantation in the state of Veracruz where her mother had worked as a cook. One day a group of Cubans had come, looking for room and board.

"They said they were from Jalisco, but we could tell they were Cubans," she explained, "because they said *chico* in between whatever they were saying. It was always *chico* this or *chico* that." Her listeners would laugh and nod their heads in recognition; they had seen Cubans portrayed in movies and they knew the idiosyncrasies of Cuban speech. They had heard comics talk with Cuban accents, just as Luz had.

"I was only a child, and sometimes I followed them out into the hills. Imagine my surprise! Do you know what they were doing there? They had guns and rifles and they crawled around on their bellies. They ran and jumped hurdles and climbed over fences." She would close her eyes, as if remembering.

"The one with the beard pulled my braids once. I was only a child, remember. 'Never tell anyone what you've seen or we'll have to shoot you', he said. He said it like a joke, but even though I was a child, I knew this was serious business.

"Juan was the name of the black one. He was the friendliest. He would sing to me and play with me.

"There was a woman, too. Her name was Haydée and I think she was the bravest person I ever met."

Luz wondered just when it was that Fidel and his men had trained in the Mexican countryside. Had she even been born then? Who cared?

In San Tomás el Grande they began to call her "comrade." They pointed her out with respect as the woman who had fought with Fidel. Some said she had never married and never would because of something that had happened back then. Batista's men were dirty pigs. "They served them to her on a plate," went the story. "Can you imagine?"

Luz didn't mind what they said. She knew people have to whisper something about a woman who has no man. Still, she hastened to set the record straight. "No, no, I never fought by his side," she said. "He was only a friend of mine, and I was very young."

But how the mighty had fallen! She had stood by Fidel's side and now she was nothing but a wage slave. In the city, Doña María talked proudly of the loyalty Luz had shown. She hadn't given the girl a raise in years and yet Luz had turned down several other offers. Some people don't know what to make of their opportunities, thought Doña María.

Luz washed the sidewalk clean in the morning; she locked up at night.

Each day brought the torture of anticipation. Luz would hear the kick and the children shouting. There were six grandchildren now. The ball would bounce and rebound and slam and crash, and a chill would slowly move up the shopgirl's spine. When the ball flew over the rail, she held her breath. It would hit the floor and roll behind the counter or into the street. The children would laugh with relief.

Behind the counter, Luz clenched her fists and waited. The ball couldn't miss forever.

Photo by Lori Burkhalter-Lackey

In the Cafeteria
Isabelle Bruder

Julia
carefully considers
being Polish and from Bayonne
for the past 79 years or more —
but now she's 84
although she looks not
one single second under 90,
speaks at length like a 20-year-old,
holds up for inspection
the ravaged opinions of her hometown —
four thousand eighty-four at the last count;

and talks
with the back of her hand
of the history and struggles
of the Polish Catholic Church
(over cinnamon danish
and grilled cheese on white)
as if it controls
every movement on earth,
and it has, even long before
she was widowed at 30
and left with four kids,
all college graduates,
one Ph.D.,

none who grew up to work
in her 50-year-old
corner candy store
which really doesn't carry
much candy anymore because
it only attracts
the riffraff and thugs...

do I have religion?
and would I mind
refilling her mug with coffee,
no sugar —
bad for the teeth.

Hideaway Inn

Virginia Rudasill Mortenson

March 1961. I was twenty-one; my sixth-grade teacher would have said, "Gloria, you're much much too old to cry." Nevertheless, three-week-old F. Scott and I had been crying nonstop for three weeks with no sign of a letup.

To make matters worse, my husband, Sid, cried too. In his last semester of a two-year junior college degree program, he was on the brink — no, actually, there was no brink to it — he was flunking. Flunking in school and in his door-to-door vacuum cleaner sales job. He was bringing in the equivalent of ten cents an hour after we paid fifty cents each for the "free" knife sets he and I (plural-pregnant tense) gave to potential customers to get his size fourteen feet inside their doors. Banging our own door, we shouted out our frustration with each other, our screaming child, and life in general. Finally, exhausted, we decided that the sales job must go before we were bankrupt and ungraduated.

No straws had to be drawn to know that it was I who must get the job. With two years of college and experience in an insurance company calculating policy loans, we figured that I shouldn't have any trouble getting a job. Wrong! First of all, I did not drive, having promised the driver's training teacher in high school that I wouldn't. Secondly, we didn't have a car anyway. Even in 1961 a ten-cents-an-hour job would not buy much twenty-five-cents-a-gallon gasoline.

Until then we hadn't needed a car. We lived across the street from the college in the former Seminary Residence. Even though the building had been converted to apartments, everyone continued to refer to it as the Seminary Residence. That title in itself meant a lot to us in righteousness status. And for fifty dollars a month, we could make do with a kitchen and a bedroom, and a shared bath down the hall, especially as the single students began moving out about the same time that Screaming F. Scott arrived. Soon we had the entire second floor to ourselves.

For all practical purposes I figured the job needed to be within walking distance and should have night hours since child care was expensive, more so I assumed, for a child who cried constantly. I reasoned that Sid could cry with F. Scott at night as he studied and I worked. I could then be free to cry with our baby during the day while Sid was in classes.

Fortunately, on the highway only four blocks away was the Hideaway Inn, in need of a waitress. Unfortunately, the job paid only forty cents an hour. "Thirty cents better than your recent job," I reminded a protesting Sid as he rocked an even more protesting F. Scott. "One of the other waitresses," I added, already including myself as a group member even though I had no previous experience, "got on the list to get hired down at Bombs for nothing per hour, zero!" Bombs was the classiest restaurant around Des Moines at the time. "It's the tips, up to a fifty a day down there if you're good."

Tips turned out to be the key word, especially after I found out that the first check would be delayed for two weeks and the cost of my uniform, twenty-five dollars, would be deducted, leaving me, if I didn't eat anything on the job, seven dollars! So, wiping away three weeks' worth of tears, I turned on a smile to rival neon flashing. "Smile for F. Scott's milk" became my motto.

I approached each of my assigned tables with the enthusiasm of a hockey fan, intent upon winning the customers over to me forever or for the rest of my waitressing career, whichever came first. Just as soon as I asked my patrons if they wanted coffee, I started a conversation; eventually I explained that I had just had a baby and that I needed money for his milk. Then, before I asked them if they wanted dessert, I always served up a sticky, sweet compliment.

By the second night the pockets of my rose-colored, unpaid for pinafore filled up to a clinking, and by seven the next morning they jingled happily as I pranced home to the Seminary Residence. F. Scott screamed his greeting, and Sid grinned sleepily as I dumped the change on our unmade bed. We counted the quarters and dimes into stacks, finally touching noses, cooing, "Ten dollars."

That initial ten dollar drop gradually swelled into a torrent of tip money for me, but with it an aridity developed around the edges of the Hideaway dining room, mummifying the experienced waitresses, especially Judy. Judy rolled her eyes up to her bleached, back-combed beehive when customers began requesting my tables. "Well, jeesee-peesee!" she mumbled her favorite expression under her breath as she directed me toward the new arrivals with her top-heavy hairdo. I always thanked her while practically skipping a circle around her to get to my guests who couldn't wait to hear all about how "little F.'s doin'," and to offer more advice on how to cure colic. Out of respect for customers, I always wrote their advice down on the back cardboard of my pad, no matter how ridiculous the ritual was that they suggested.

Within four weeks I had the entire Saturday night square dance crowd as well as the Monday night bowlers requesting my tables. Not only that but what I called the up-and-up salesmen, the ones not looking for any outside marital recreation, asked for me with regularity. One of my favorites, Bozo, he liked to call himself, always left me five dollars, even if he only had a cup of coffee. "You remind me of my daughter," he said, winking.

Every time he left, Judy imitated Bozo's wink to me. "Here's five for F. And we all know what F stands for!" She surprised me since we named our son after F. Scott Fitzgerald, the great writer, Sid being an English major and all, and even Sid himself didn't know what the F stood for. But, not wanting to make any waves with Judy because of the certain shipwreck to follow if I did, I zipped my lips and trod water. Besides, she stopped winking at me soon enough after her false upper eyelashes got stuck to the lower ones and she spent about an hour of her shift in a permanent wink.

Soon Judy had more to think about than winking anyway. She was moving up on the list for Bombs. "I'm up to seven now," Judy said the night after Pinky and Birdie quit in anticipation of being called; they were numbers one and two on the Bomb's list. "I'll be number two in a couple of weeks," she said loud enough for Jim, the manager, to hear.

"I got news for you. You're already number two," he mumbled. I didn't know how Jim found out, but I'm sure Judy didn't hear him. I would have told her the good news myself, if one of my best customers hadn't sat down right then at table 1, my table, without even being ushered in by the hostess. Later, when I saw Judy, I forgot all about telling her because in the meantime Jim called me into his office to let me know what a great job I was doing and could I possibly work a double shift on the weekends once in a while on account of a couple more waitresses on days as well as two more cooks were also quitting. I told him that I would have to consult with Sid since I wasn't sure about his schedule. Then, to stay on his good side, I added, "I don't know how much of F. Scott Sid can take even if he is an English major." I laughed but Jim didn't. I don't think he got the joke. Maybe he hadn't ever taken American Lit.

When Sid said that I could work for one or two double shifts, I didn't know whether to be happy for the chance to make more in tips or sad because of being dead tired. All that smiling like a clown was wearing me out along with not getting much sleep during the day with F. Scott still raging, despite doctor and customer "cures." But I was averaging seventeen dollars a night in tips now; on a double shift I could probably count on up to thirty. I decided to give it a try. I wish I had thought of that famous saying, "Pride goeth before a fall." Then, again, maybe it's just as well I didn't remember to think of it because I realize now that it doesn't quite fit the situation anyhow. The fall part is right on, but the word greed should have been in there.

With my mind zeroing in on all the money I would be earning, I rushed into Jim's office with "Yes!" practically falling off my lips, ready to agree to whatever he asked me to do. "You'll work Saturday night and stay on to work all day Sunday then?" Jim beamed.

Consenting to Jim's schedule was actually my second mistake. My first was not checking the calendar ahead of time. Sunday was Mother's Day.

F. Scott and I cried a more poignant duet than usual when we discovered at the same moment that I would be smiling, serving, slaving for other mothers and their children on my first Mother's Day as a mother. "I don't see what the big deal is," Sid said. I cried harder. F. Scott cried harder.

Luckily, my own mother who lived in Austin sent me a glittery rhinestone pin that spelled MOTHER in big letters. As I attached MOTHER to my pinafore Saturday night before I went into action, I felt better. At least all the patrons, even the ones I could not wait on, would know the sacrifice I was making, especially on Sunday, by being there with them.

Judy failed to see my point. "You'd better take that thing off your uniform right now before management sees it. Don't you know Hideaway's rule about jewelry on uniforms?"

"I'm wearing it, no matter what," I said. I felt unusually tired, yet energetic; weak but strong. "Since when have you cared about Hideaway rules?" I noticed the wadded-up hairnet that she usually attached like a rose into her beehive was missing; a hairnet was required. I didn't have to say anything about it since I saw that she saw what I was looking for and not seeing.

"I'm just telling you, you'll be in trouble. Just wait."

I wanted to tell Judy: No, you just wait. You'll be a mother some day too. You're jealous of me, jealous because I have earned the right to wear this pin.

But the moment was gone. And the dining room was full even at eleven, probably late-night travelers trying to reach their mothers before tomorrow, I thought. Switching on my smile was harder with sixteen hours ahead of me, sixteen hours of waiting for people to decide on exactly what they wanted to eat at that particular moment: "Let's see. What am I hungry for tonight?" many questioned themselves out loud while I humored them as though they were my children. "Hamburger, french fries, chocolate malt? Or how about a dinner? Chicken? Steak?" I wanted to shout, How would you like slop, Pigs? But, I caught myself, Tips! Smile! "Milk for the little one to drink? I have a little boy too. He likes milk just like you do. That's why his mama has to work, to pay for his milk. What's your name? Jeff is a nice name. My little boy's named F. Scott. He's just a baby. You're a big boy, Jeff. If you clean up your plate tonight, I'll bring you a balloon. OK? What a cutie he is!"

By the time the square dancers arrived at two—later than usual because of an apparent birthday celebration, judging by the pointed paper hats—my back already ached from carrying loaded trays and bending to scoop up handfuls of lettuce from the salad drawer and rolls from an even lower oven drawer.

"Hey, little F.'s mom! C'mere!"

"Over here, Honey! Don't pay no attention to those yahoos."

"Start here, Darlin'. We got the Birthday Boy with us."

As if I had been called to center stage at the beginning of a performance, I feigned delight at being there at their service and acted bewildered at having to choose one table over another. "I love you all," I said to the group wearing red to match their bloodshot eyes. "But the Birthday Boy is at this table and he must come first."

"He comes first all right, Darlin'. When he comes, that is, but he's gettin' so old that he don't come much anymore!"

"Wilbur Ray Hopp! I'm ashamed of you, talkin' like that to this sweet child." The elastic neck of the woman's red peasant blouse was pulled down, revealing her right shoulder.

"Don't 'sweet child' me. She's got a mother pin on, ain't she? She's the one that Bobretta told us about what babbles on a mile a minute about her kid named F. Hey, Bobretta! This the one with the F kid?"

"His name's F. Scott after the famous writer. I'm working to earn money to buy his milk while my husband finishes college." Careful! Careful! Don't lose the tip! Obnoxious, inconsiderate drunks! My stomach churned with rage.

But, minutes later I was running to the kitchen as usual, shouting out my orders to the cook, grabbing handfuls of salad and glopping on the dressing. My own throat was dry as I listened and watched the fountain drinks swishing over the ice cubes in the glasses. I licked my lips and swallowed. Maybe, I'd buy a waffle after the first shift, I teased myself; drown the whole thing in strawberry syrup. But I knew I wouldn't. Not once since I'd started at the Hideaway had I spent any money for food. I hadn't stolen any food either as I had seen others do, including Judy. I always pretended I didn't like to eat.

By seven with the sun shining the way it should on Mother's Day, I was more exhausted than I could ever remember being. When Jim motioned me to his office, my heart did a joyful flip, hoping he would tell me to go on home. Instead, he pointed at my MOTHER pin. "I won't fine you this time, Gloria, but didn't you remember that jewelry is not to be worn on the uniform?"

174

"How about if I just go on home now? I'm too tired to stay for another shift anyway."

"Not now. Not after you committed yourself last week. It's too late. I couldn't get a replacement. Just be a good girl; remove the pin and get back to work."

As I removed the MOTHER pin and put it in my pocket with the tips, I could feel the tears gathering for a storm inside my body. I walked out with no words. And no smile. No matter how hard I tried that morning to smile, I could not force it back to my face. Order after order became automatic without any extra comments and few tips. I felt like I was drifting on a cloud with no say in where I was going.

"What's the matter with you, Smiley?" Judy was actually joking with me as she poured maple syrup into glass pitchers on a tray. For the first time I could tell she was tired too; dark rings surrounded her eyes. She was working a sixteen-hour shift with me. "You'll perk up in about a half an hour. Just wait. That's when the loving mothers and their loving families come waltzing in here and act like hateful monsters to us. Busiest day in the restaurant business and the most demanding. Jim's a slave driver, making us work a double today."

Judy was right. But as wise as I began to see she was in her predictions, she could never have prepared either one of us for what happened in the busiest hour of the busiest of all restaurant days. Mother's Day at twelve noon, May 1961. With every table surrounded by occupied chairs and a waiting area stuffed with hungry children and frazzled parents, suddenly, without warning, the cook ripped off his white hat and apron. Screaming "I quit!" he ran out the back door, leaving the huge grill covered with every type of steak imaginable in every stage of cooking.

Shocked, I stared at Judy. "What are we going to do?"

"Do?" She smiled at me. "Looks like we're gonna be doin' some cookin'." She bounded over to the grill and grabbed the tongs. "Let's see. My fillets...these must be your strips..."

I gulped. "Well, nobody told me that cooks can't wear jewelry." I rescued MOTHER from my pocket of tips and stuck it back on the pinafore. Suddenly, I felt one hundred percent better. "Might as well tell 'em the truth." I glanced out the kitchen door porthole into the packed dining room, full of squirming children banging their spoons, throwing crackers on the floor, circling the tables and their proud mothers. "Sympathy will be with us. It'll be a great tip-maker. Please bear with us. Since the cook just quit, we'll be cooking your meal as well as serving it, just like home, huh?"

Judy laughed. I laughed, a sincere laugh, my first sincere anything at the Hideaway.

If it hadn't been for Judy I don't think I ever would have survived that afternoon. She even made me a waffle "For free!" and soaked it in strawberry syrup. "Eat it," she demanded when I protested about my customers—my tips. "Gloria, you're much much too skinny! You're beginning to look like a tip!" She sounded a lot like my sixth-grade teacher, who hadn't taught me nearly as much about life and work, humor and honesty in a year as Judy had in a few hours.

Actually, Mother's Day weekend was my last at the Hideaway. With splotches of strawberry syrup and MOTHER glaring across my chest, I planted myself in front of Jim at the end of my shift. "I quit! I'm going to learn how to drive."

As I walked out of Hideaway for the last time, Judy honked. "Want a lift?" Happy to get home to Sid and F. Scott quicker with my news, I hopped into Judy's green '54 Chevy.

"You know, Gloria, you're really not such a Miss Goody Two-Shoes as I thought. Where do you live?"

"In the Seminary Residence across from the college."

"I might a known! Hey, did I tell ya? I'm goin' to Bombs!"

Anyhow, that Mother's Day turned out perfectly after all. When I got home and picked F. Scott up from his crib, he smiled at me for the first time. And, come to think of it, most of his life since he's been smiling sincere smiles; so have I.

Woolworth Lunch

Denise Bergman

Liver & onions & eggs
rings like the chant
in the *Wizard of Oz*
on the cardboard sign
with an hourglass Coke
The price circled
is a dollar sixty-five
Linda hands platters
liver & onions & eggs
to the Wednesday crowd
She slides catsup
down the counter
totals the checks
and wipes coffee spills
all with the speed of one
who knows lunch
is a worker's only hour
The floor waxer knows
He moves
to buff a distance away
and the saleswoman knows
She tunes the radio dial
She lifts the volume
They ask for easy listening
no weather and certainly
no news

Flowers of Saturday Night

Eileen Malone

One gets used to it, serving rum drinks
every Saturday night to exotic flowers
gathered at little tables, mirrored
vanilla orchids, hibiscus, hybrids
that toss and nod in winds of music.

"Please ask me to dance,"
she doesn't say, slanting a smile.
A blossom secured, she unfurls creepers,
gives hope time to take root,
lights a cigarette, drops petal
after petal in shivers and giggles.

"Would you like to dance?"
he doesn't move his bright wet lips,
a sullen salt-watered sailor
visits, browses, sniffs about,
a pirate regarding floral treasure,
his ship resting not far off.

One gets used to it, the abundance
of seabirds blowing into our rain
forest heat, plunging beaks into our
confined flowers, pecking, cracking seeds,
spitting out bits of stigmas.

One gets tired of knowing too much
finds a small table, a dark corner,
drinks rum, watches flowers try to dance
to the sound of foreign wings that beat,
every Saturday night they beat,
oh yes, beat, one gets used to it.

Blanca Cats

Penny Gasaway

The white girls come, the white girls come
down to Central Avenue from Sunset and Bel Air:
sweet blanca cats dragging their furs behind them
on the concrete walks they range freely through
the preserve from Alabam past Dunbar to the Down Beat
moving to seductive rhythms, prowling for dark meat;
high heeled, well heeled, painted and perfumed
traps lightly sprung, oh, lightly sprung —
the smell ripe upon them and the prey close sniffing around.
blanca cats, blonde, blue-eyed predators parading in the night
coup counters bearing notched whips, the proof of many kills
moaning and mewing a question one to the other
         was it good?

Makeover

Joan Maiers

His hands were moving across my face almost like an
artist on a canvas.
    —Model Marla Hanson, testifying about being
      slashed with a razor blade, *Newsweek*, June 1986

Photographer's model
turns up her collar,
puts cold drafts aside
for warmer quarters.
What she needs
to pull her through
is one stiff drink.
She who tipped
full fifteen percent,
knows her market value
dropped to new lows.

Even the animal pelts
silky to the eyes and touch
command the once-over.
She wants to be easy
on the eyes, asks, make me
feel new. She wants
some color, gelée to cancel
pinched muscle tone
design left by hit-and-run
primitive artist.

Her face now
moves in sections.
City meets jungle edge,
glides past day's
revolving doors.

Take This Job And
Kathryn Daniels

Well, I told *him* all right! You should have seen me! Took the wad of bills out of my pocket and slapped it in his hand, dumped the change too, a huge handful, so big some of it spilled on the cement. "Here's your money, take it! I've had it with this shit! You're nothing but a goddamn lackey, and if you weren't so pathetic, I'd feel sorry for you!" Yeah, I did, I said that to him. Then I went into the office and took the uniform off right there and threw it on the ground. I did that especially to piss him off, because he'd told me before I should go into the bathroom to change like the other quote unquote girls. The guys can take their shirts off in the office but us women—pardon me, us *girls!*—have to go hide ourselves in the two-by-four bathroom lest we offend someone's precious eyes (read: male!). Well, fuck that shit!

So what happened was, there was this big long line of cars waiting at every pump, and people were getting kind of testy. It was nice and sunny out—hot, humid, one of those scorchers—and those cars were putting out a lot of fumes. Listen, I actually still *like* the smell of gas, believe it or not, but all that exhaust floating around—full of carbon dioxide and all—is something else. My lungs had been starting to bother me recently and I'd read this article about how dangerous gasoline fumes can be for your health, how they can give you brain damage and stuff. Now that's scary! Regular air is bad enough! Anyways, when the boss just happened to be on vacation, I put the article on the bulletin board in the office—you know, I believe people should know what they're getting themselves into—and when he got back, it mysteriously disappeared. Too bad, it was my only copy. Later I heard it through the grapevine that he didn't appreciate my thoughtfulness too much. Well, *some*one has to look out for us! The oil companies sure aren't going to.

In order to try and save my lungs a bit, I started asking customers if they'd mind turning off their engines when I knew they'd have a long wait for gas. Most everybody was nice enough and obliged without a fuss. I guess they sort of felt sorry for me, having to pump gas for a living, being outside in all kinds of foul weather, and having to breathe those nasty fumes. And then being a *girl* on top of it all! If one more person said to me, "What's a nice girl like you doing in a place like this?," I thought I'd hit them over the head with the pump nozzle. What did they think I was doing there—playing tiddlywinks? I was doing what many of my coworkers were doing—just another Women's Studies alumna eking out a meager living.

Don't feel sorry for me, now. The truth is, when I graduated, I got the job of my dreams. I *wanted* to pump gas! It was the first job I applied for, and I got it! I was satisfied. My brain was so tired, I wanted to give it a rest. I wanted my *body* to get a workout for a change! And did it get a workout! Running around to all those different cars, timing everything just right—four dollars regular here, two dollars unleaded there, an oil check over there—in all kinds of weather. And trying to treat the customers right, too! Believe me, there's nothing like running around in a pair of wet, oily sneakers to challenge your sense of humor! But I got into it—wearing a white uniform with a green stripe running down my leg, watching my soft hands turn scratchy and calloused and cleaning them with chemical goo, my arms growing hard and my pale skin turning tan. I loved taking the readings, doing inventory on the oil cans, making my money balance. The customers could be all right, too—one guy used to drop me by a bagel with cream cheese when I worked alone early Sunday mornings. And the women I worked with—they were mostly women—were something else! Dora, a photographer, with sticking-up black hair and blue eyes you could die for; tall Jill who wanted to be a lawyer but could easily be a comedian. Then there was the woman who rode up one day on a Harley and demanded to see the boss, saying she wanted a job. "What's your name?" I asked. "Natasha," she said, freeing her long black hair from the helmet. "That's a beautiful name," I said, swallowing hard. "Yes," she said. "I know."

No, I wasn't sorry at all. But while getting minimum wage was one thing I had consented to, taking abuse wasn't part of the plan.

So it was broiling out that day, as I said. Patience was wearing thin all around, and the air was polluted as hell. I asked a few people to shut off

184

their engines—no problem. Then I went up to this guy in a white Lincoln Continental and tapped on the tinted window. He had one of those electric window gizmos and buzzed it down. "Yes?" he asked, not too kindly.

"Sir, would you mind shutting off your engine while you wait? It's going to take a little while."

He gave me a look to kill and said, "As a matter of fact, I do!"

"Oh, forget it then," I said, and walked away.

Damn, I felt pissed. What's the big deal to him? But OK, it's his right to say no, just like it's my right to ask.

Next thing I know, he's standing beside me, I can feel his presence and I know it's him without looking. I'm not looking because I'm helping someone else. But as soon as I'm done, I turn to him and say, "Yes?" and I can see right away that it's downhill from there but there's nothing I can do to stop it.

"Why did you ask me that?" he says.

"Because the fumes are hazardous to my health, that's why," I say.

Then he goes, "Well, I didn't come here to worry about your health."

I'm getting real heated up now. "Fine. Maybe you didn't, but *I* have to. It's *my* lungs."

Then he says, "Well if you don't like it, then why don't you get another job?"

In that moment, I learned what seeing red means. Here's this guy sitting in a shiny white Lincoln Continental with the air conditioning going full blast telling me if I don't like pumping gas, to get another job—like it's so easy in this two-bit college/farming town, overrun with overqualified overeducated professional lifetime students! If you want a simple job in Fotomat, you need a Ph.D. in Photography, for christ's sake. And by that time, the fun of pumping gas was wearing off; it had ceased to be a choice. It was getting to be winter, and I was ready for something serious, a job where I could flex the brains I'd spent years—to say nothing of dollars—exercising. But I couldn't find diddlysquat. Just like the women I worked with—talented artists, activists, potential lawyers—all caught up in the middle of an employment crisis. We're struggling our butts off to keep our morale up, to maintain our visions — and this *jerk* in a white Lincoln has the balls to say to me, "Then why don't you get another job?"

So I said to him the only thing I could possibly say under the circumstances. I said, "Fuuuck you!"

Let me tell you, the look on his face was worth every minute of it. He was so shocked, he could barely talk. He started mumbling under his breath, "I can't believe you said that! I can't believe a *lady* said that to me!" He kept repeating it, saying it louder and more wounded and angry each time.

Well, I lost it by then. My mouth was on automatic pilot. I looked him square in his beady eyes and I yelled, "I never said I was a *lady! I'm a woman!* A *woman!*"

We were attracting a regular audience. About that time, the jerk demanded to see the manager. "Certainly," I said. "I'd be glad to get him for you."

The manager — a little blonde brownnose, younger than me even, a real ROTC type — calmed him down as best he could. As soon as the guy split, the manager wanted to hear the whole story and he was fine, he was with me, until I got to the part where I said "Fuck you."

"Jackie," he said, the way my mother used to when I did something wrong. "You *know* you shouldn't have said that."

"Hey, easy for you say, Joe," I said. "You have no idea the abuse us girls take out there."

"Look, I do know, but that's no excuse for speaking to a customer that way."

He went off to ponder the universe and do his managerial thing. Meanwhile all my friends crowded around me, offering support. They were proud of me, they said; that guy was an asshole, he deserved it, I should try to stay calm.

Then, lo and behold, the white Lincoln reappeared! The sucker came back without his wife to insure that my ass was grass! He told the punk boss that he wanted me fired, or he'd sue the company for libel. He kept looking over at me, surrounded by my womanfriends, giving me an I'll-get-you-if-it's-the-last-thing-I-do kind of look.

So as soon as he took off, the manager went over to the pay phone to call the Big Boss. I had half-hoped he wouldn't, but I expected he would. The managers they hire for companies like that are always rats; it's part of the job description.

He hung up the phone and stood there a minute, like he was undergoing an existential dilemma or something. Then he came over to me and said, "Jackie, I hate to do it, but you'll have to leave. Give me your money." The gas station's money, he meant. We carried hundreds on us at a time.

Well, I tell you, in that second my mind flashed back to a TV show I used to watch when I was a kid: "Branded." Do you remember it? Chuck Connors is in the Army or something, Civil War, I think, and he gets disbarred or excommunicated or whatever they call it in the service. What happens is they rip the stripes off his shoulders and the badges off his chest. It's quiet, the only sound you hear. Very dramatic. Or that's how I remember it anyway. It made my heart sink every time. You could tell it was the worst thing that could happen to a person, the lowest of the low.

Of course this wasn't the worst thing that could happen to me. I mean, a woman has to make a living but she does have to have some pride. So that's when I slapped the money into his hand, told him off, and went into the office and stripped. My coworkers said they wanted to quit in sympathy but they couldn't afford to. Then I got on my bicycle and rode away, and I didn't look back. I knew everyone stood watching me go.

Sometimes when I meet people and tell them this story — and I do tell it even though it makes my adrenaline skyrocket — they say, "Oh, it was you who did that? I've heard about you!" So I've become a legend in my own time. Not bad, huh? People say I'll look back and laugh about it someday. I can't wait. Because being a legend won't pay the bills. Meanwhile, what am I gonna do about work?

Piece Work
Mona Elaine Adilman

The knot of women,
heat-shrivelled,
hunch over their machines —
piece work puppets
manipulating bits
of fabric, the whir
and hum of technology
stinging the air
like a giant wasp.

Steam iron in hand,
the girl from Barbados,
soaked in sweat,
dreams of the sea.
The hissing iron distorts
her crested vision
with a vaporous
river of sound.

Dialects in Greek,
Portuguese and Italian
are savory fruits
in the sweltering
factory heat.
Conversation rises
like yeast
in the industrious
oven of humanity.

Pockets, collars, sleeves,
in rainbow streams,
flow from each
punctuating needle.
Buffeting
buttonhole machines
bite sharply
into polyester tissue.
Precision speaks
with geologic force.

The factory is canopied with
plastic-swathed garments,
candy-cane copies
of haute-couture originals.
Operators, cutters,
pressers, shippers
scurry across
the room, hunchbacked,
ducking under 4 foot high
metal pipes
supporting parades
of dresses and slack suits,
labelled, tagged,
inspected,
ready to be shipped.

In the show room,
air conditioners
articulate
a comforting chill.
Buyers
finger the goods,
and eye the models.
The designer
is all smiles.
The boss has
order forms
at the ready.
The season looks
promising.

In the factory,
the odor of sweat
mingles with the smell
of steaming garments
and dry-cleaning fluid,
but the women
are lucky to be working,
and live in fear
of seasonal
layoffs.

The needle trade
marches on,
populated by
its human machines.
Immigrant women,
shapeless
in sleeveless smocks,
are mechanical tools,
overexposed film

      hemming, pressing, basting,
      threading, cutting, stitching.

The fashion treadmill
goes round and round
on the laws of
supply and demand.

Production
is an adrenalin flow,
a cover-up for
yesterday's cop-out,
today's emptiness,
the lost look of tomorrow.

Piece work is the
name of the game.

    Pieces of soul.

        Pieces of bone.

           Pieces of sinew.

               Pieces of gut.

                   Pieces of pride.

               Pieces of pain.

           Pieces of flesh.

        Pieces of people.

    Pieces of profit...

        PIECE WORK.

The Radium Girls

Barbara Unger

She doesn't mind talking about hers
the slow kind   bruises and swellings
an epidemic of tumors   more photos
nubile girls in cloche hats
wall-eyed boas   grinning at the camera

Radium dial factory girls   deft of hand
each proud to be a woman   earning a man's paycheck
painting numbers   that glow in the dark
on our bedroom clocks   as the time clock ticks
their tractable faces   white and luminous
as calla lilies   bending bobbed heads
over their handiwork   licking the pearly tips
to stub their brushes   to a fine point

In this new element   distilled from deep underground
in the moist rich earth   promising miracle cures
and healing waters   each one unaware
she offers   a share in her body   a note to come due
in five years or ten   down the line

In the X-ray room   she crouches on an iron table
in the government study   the Army needs to see
her shining ribs   her spine like organ keys

More photos   boarded-up factories
steel coffins   barely muffle
the radiant ticking below   negative numbers
half-lives poisoned   an empty clock face
its nights and days   burned away

Sixty years later   this Midwestern grave
of the last of the red-hot mommas
still too hot to handle

Marilyn McCusker: Coal Miner

Savina A. Roxas

Newspapers told of how
she won the fight to descend the shaft
like men to earn nine-fifty an hour.

Two years she worked below
in a dirty, dark, rat-infested pit,
sticking bolts in holes overhead
to secure the roof over the deep dirt bed.

The day that tremors shook the mine
old timers yelled, "The roof's working,"
ran like hell and made it out.
But Marilyn froze in place.

Not like a moth that moves toward light
she hugged the dark instead
where airless pockets one by one
snuffed out her vital spark.
An old statistic for the men
a new one she became.

Newspapers told of how
she lost her life, underground,
like a man
earning nine-fifty an hour.

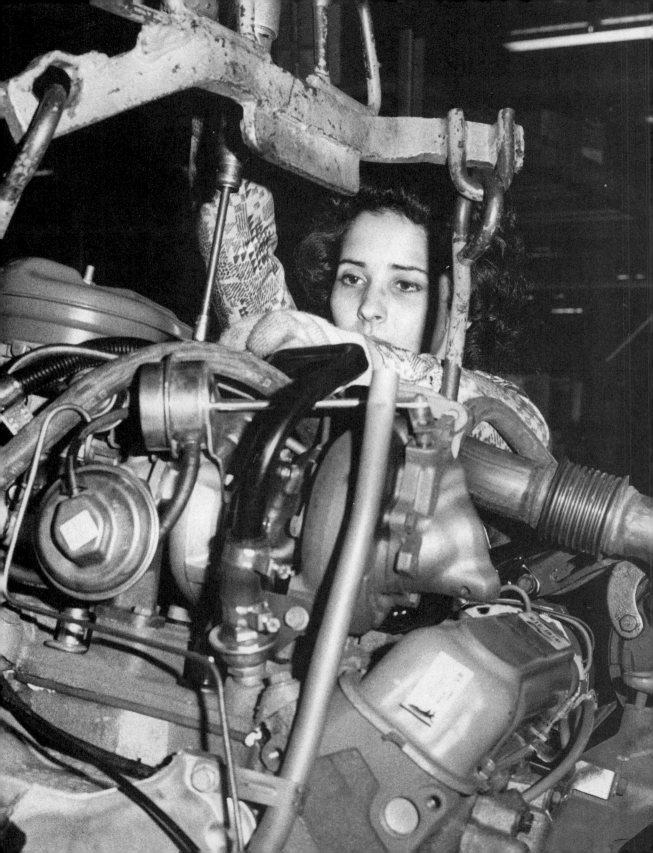

The Tomato Packing Plant Line
Enid Shomer

Bumped and rolling jovially
down the conveyor the tomatoes
dance in   a press of faces
the shine on their skins like smiles
the stem ends chipper as cowlicks.

Young women remove the mistakes —
harelips   two-headed ones   gashed ones
with papery crosshatched scars.
Tiny ones too are removed
to be juiced with the freaks.

At the far end hemmed in by boxes
the old women sort the tomatoes
the largest and the perfect ones first.
Their hands   like their eyes
know the swell before ripeness.
It is something they flaunted
on Fridays   a gust that inflated
box-pleated skirts into bells
as they stepped into dusk
hands washed white of tomatoes
which did not survive
their ripeness.

Las Lechuzas

Jacklyn Potter

Las lechuzas *are like eagles and owls. At night women we know become*
lechuzas. *We can stop the curse only if we say:* "Sal y pimienta, pimienta
y sal." *We say it and* la lechuza *falls from the sky. Then she cannot curse
us or harm us.*
                          —Migrant farmworker, Eastern Shore of Virginia

Your hands move   among the brightnesses
of growing tomatoes, peppers,
babies from your own
ripeness.

You bend   and sweat   and scratch
the yellow dust   that makes
a folding   and unfolding map
of your forehead.

I travel the paths   I see there
along the tiny arteries   that end
as sharply as your fingers snap
the fruit   leaving blunt stems
pointing at sky dusk.

I bring no song.
Women, you have your own.
You sing it   in the bare light
of a migrant camp light bulb. You sing it
in narrow compartments   behind screen
doors that frame an ancient shaft of light
your husbands and sons follow
to work at the ketchup factory.

Rise your moon
Rise *las lechuzas*
above fields   above the night rows
where green is black
where women speak wings
where women look down
on smaller moons   that hang
beneath black leaves.

Lechuzas above me   delicious fear
¡Sal y pimienta   pimienta y sal!
A sovereign belief spells my hunger
as I move   down Safeway rows
choosing.

la lechuza [Spanish]: owl; farmworkers apply word to a spiritually and
physically powerful woman, who can fly and curse weaker beings
below — she   loses her powers only by the ritual of spoken language
chanted by those weaker beings on earth.

Photo by Clytia Fuller

Hands

Mildred Barker

The crowded bus comes to a stop. Cannery workers ooze out its narrow door and regroup on the coarsely gravelled asphalt. Being new, Rosa Romera does not know the other women, but she quietly keeps near the center of the group, surrounded by the noise of the others, moving when they move. With one hand she clutches the string handles of the shopping bag which holds her personal belongings. With the other hand she rearranges a loose strand of hair to cover a scar on her cheek.

Staying close together, the women move through the vast area of warehouses. As they move, they make an eager, busy sound. Together they pass the brewery. Together they flow out around a truck that is unloading in the street. One of the women points to a man walking along the tracks, and giggles loudly. Two trucks loaded high with tomatoes roar past. "Hooray!" the women shout, waving.

The women cross the tracks together. Rosa is one of them. They flow into the brilliant light of the cannery to take the place of the last shift.

Rosa is assigned a place on the line, and goes to it. The great belt with its load of fruit moves down the line, a river of tomatoes. The floor vibrates under Rosa's feet. She is part of the vibration. She cuts the tomatoes as they come. No matter how fast she cuts, or how slowly, the fruit keeps coming. Hands on both sides of the belt snatch the tomatoes. Forty hands snatch and cut so fast, hands and fruit blur together. Hurry! Faster!

The woman next to Rosa cuts furiously, as if she is trying to kill something before it kills her. Rosa watches the lightning movements, and tries to make her knife flash and cut as quickly. The hard handle of the knife hits against a callus on her hand with each sharp stroke.

Above Rosa's head a maze of belts conveys thousands of shiny new cans. Some empty, some without lids, some with uncooked fruit, they go from one machine to another or to the packing room, or to and from the warehouse. Infinite lines of cans descend noisily from the ceiling along intricate paths carefully laid out for them. If any fall off, Rosa does not see them. The system seems perfect.

To one side, men are shoving machines about, trying to make room for more equipment on the crowded floor. There is no room for anything not needed.

Water gushes from an open valve. Finding no convenient drain, it floods the concrete floor. Rosa feels it flowing around her feet and slowly seeping into her shoes. She keeps working. Faster! She must keep her place on the line. The muscles in her neck tighten. Her fingers have stopped aching. They are numb and stiff. She wipes the sweat from her forehead with the back of a tomato-stained hand.

Across from her another young woman is cutting tomatoes, and the gold hoops dangling from her ears sway and flash with every movement of her hands. They are exactly like the earrings Rosa's sister, Laura, wore.

It has been nearly a year since Rosa, with her brothers and sisters, left their mother in the County Hospital at Stockton, and took the special hospital bus back. They knew their mother was dying, but there was no work near Stockton then, and they could not wait. Like a cluster of thistle seeds blown apart in the wind, they dispersed. Anna went to work in a packing shed, Julio to fight a forest fire in the Sierra Madre, and Laura just disappeared. Rosa has not heard from them since. She has covered many miles looking for work, drifting with the crops. For picking fruit, no machine is as gentle as the human hand, and Rosa follows the fruit harvests, offering her two hands, moving from cherries to apricots to peaches.

Now the tomatoes, smooth and abundant, pour onto the line. The air is humid and heavy with the odor of crushed fruit. Where the steam hoses have failed to reach, bits of moldy fruit cling tenaciously and add a faint mustiness.

Soon the crop will dwindle. There will be fewer and fewer trucks roaring up to the cannery. One by one, workers will be laid off, the slower ones first; then, one day, all at once, the whole plant will close down, and the season will be over.

Cut. Cut. Cut. Keep moving the knife. Do not think.

The search for work will begin again, up and down the long, wide valleys of California, the constant moving to so many places one forgets where one has lived. Cut. Cut. . .

"Where was I born?" Rosa asked her mother. Her mother tightened her lips and kept working.

"Don't you know?" Rosa persisted. "Was it during hop picking? Was it near the cucumber fields or in the orange groves?"

"I'm not sure," her mother answered. "It's all run together."

They were cutting apricots then, and her mother added, "Here, take this bucket of pits and empty it."

The hand reaching out to Rosa was deeply wrinkled and raw. After years of bending too long over the crops, Rosa's mother could not straighten her back. Her shoulders remained hunched forward, her hands held in front of her, ready always to continue working. Except for a swollen belly, her stooped body was lean and bony.

When Rosa's mother spoke, it was usually of Mexico and the home on a mountainside Rosa had never seen. It was as if the more than twenty years Rosa's mother had spent wandering over California with her growing family were but a dream that could vanish like smoke from a smudge pot.

"In Mexico the dead are carried away slowly on foot, not rushed away in cars."

"In Mexico the sky is clear, and the clouds are separate, not smeared together."

Sometimes she would talk about Rosa's father and the looms he once had: "In Mexico your father was always weaving—beautiful rugs, and no two ever alike. I wish you could have seen. He wove late every night, burning the kerosene lamp. I used to sit and watch his hands."

When the river dried, her parents had left their home, taking everything with them that they could carry. The heavy loom had to be left behind.

The woman next to Rosa elbows her now. "Better get busy," she says. "The foreman is walking this way."

At the other end of the room, the buzz of the press begins, the machine that squeezes and mashes fruit into pulp. Rosa shudders. She hates machines that chop, cut, or crush. She was about ten years old when she heard the scream and saw the machine and her father. With one hand he was reaching out to free the hand that was caught; then, suddenly, both hands were held fast. Someone turned off the machine, and her father ran away from it, his hands held up to his face, laughing loudly.

It is all right, Rosa remembers thinking. The horrible thing did not happen. It was all a joke, and he is laughing.

Her father never worked again. His crushed hands did not heal, and something inside him seemed crushed and broken, too. He sat all day, and did not speak or eat.

Then, one evening, he seemed better. His face was flushed, but his eyes focused brightly. "Where is my loom?" he asked. "I have a new design, greater than anything I have ever seen. I have to get started. Now."

"You will have your loom," Rosa's mother assured him, not looking at his broken hands.

By morning Rosa's father had lost consciousness. All that day he spoke only once, but no one could understand what he was saying, and sometime that night — they never knew at what moment — he died.

The foreman taps Rosa's shoulder, and hands her a pink slip. She holds the paper, and looks at it. There is no need to read; she knows what it means. One reddened hand closes tightly about the bit of stiff paper. She cannot open her hand. The jagged bit seems grown fast to it. Unconsciously her other hand goes to her cheek, and slides down slowly. "I will work faster," she shouts above the roar of the machines.

"Sorry," he says, "but that's it."

The movement of the wheels does not stop. "Get out. Get out," the machines pound all the rest of the day. Finally the shift ends, and Rosa is paid for her work. By the door she passes a barrel full of crumpled cans, the rejects that have fallen or been caught and smashed.

Outside she walks with the other workers, as though still one of them. They chat happily. She is silent. She wishes she had left earlier, alone. It is not until she has gotten on the bus with the others and found a seat that she realizes she has no idea where she will get off.

Unemployment Poem

Lorraine Schein

I have joined the ranks of the unemployed.
We work at watching the moon come up.
We're unstable too ugly too old to work;
Our job is making the air circulate.

A Wellesley Girl

Toni de Bonneval

There are days, Maura thought, when you know that everything is going to be all right. The kids call it vibes. It's the feeling you have when you wake up and want to get up, want to move. When she had dieted regularly, she had called it a thin day. On such mornings, scales weren't necessary, she was simply thin. Today was like that—not a thin day—just a good day.

Sydney Omarr had said: "Saturn is in the descendant. A bad place is passed. A good day for business contacts."

"Thank you, Sydney," said Maura fervently. "Thank you."

The trick to job hunting is that you must have confidence. If you know, they know. She knew.

Shortly after Maura got on the bus, a young man rose and offered her his seat. He might be twenty years her junior, but no one gives his seat to a woman anymore unless she's old, and there was no way not to see the gesture as incipiently flirtatious. Certainly she didn't intend to make anything of it, but it was flattering, a good sign.

She looked out the window. The hard winter grass that poked sharply through the snow along the slopes on either side of the turnpike had grown tediously familiar in the past four months, but today a thin, soft drizzle was melting all the snow, and spring was coming.

Maura reviewed her schedule. At one o'clock there was the appointment at Pierce-Martin, the publishing house. The job was for a copy editor. She would have preferred more responsibility. Nonetheless the offer provided a pleasant security, and it wasn't as if she were committed. Before the appointment she would have plenty of time to explore two other places, and perhaps, if things were going well, she would have time for a nice lunch.

At 8:35 the bus came to a belching stop. Maura stepped off briskly and plunged into the tunnel to make the connection with the Red Line to Park Square. After a single stop, she got off the Red Line and hurried up the stairs to make the final connection for Copley.

As her head came level with the top stair, she saw an already half-full car still taking on passengers. Instinctively she took the last few steps at a rush and, hurrying past the newsstand, inserted herself in the throng pushing toward the trolley. Her nose pressed against the plaid woolen back of a college student. To her left, a black woman with a briefcase eased forward, but Maura twisted in such a way that the next surge shifted her ahead of the woman and to the side of the boy in the woolen jacket. However, when she was not more than four people from the trolley, Maura suddenly changed her mind. If the doors were to close directly in front of her, it would be an undeniable downer. Pulling her shoulders inward, she let the others push by. Loose of the throng, Maura drew in a deep breath. The trolley doors closed folding in their brood. Promptly, from the other side another car appeared. Her face relaxed into a grin. She had made the right decision. "Today," she hummed exultantly, finding a seat on the empty second trolley, "today is the first day of the rest of your life."

Maura had selected John Hancock Insurance for her first interview. The building, dropped like a silver slab in the center of the Back Bay, reminded her of the monolith in the beginning of *2001*. When George had left her for Nessa, he hadn't taken the VCR, and just last week she'd watched the movie again. It made her laugh now to think this silver slab might contain her future.

As she crossed the bright glamour of the lobby and stepped into the elevator, Maura's spirits were high. The company advertised continual employment possibilities and training programs, so experience wasn't a must.

Ms. Hart, the personnel representative, was round, crisp, pleasant, and not so many years younger than Maura. She sat behind a round, bare table and examined the application papers thoroughly before looking up.

"Your volunteer work with the PTA and with the Suburban-Urban Coalition for the Homeless is not only admirable but valuable," said Ms. Hart at last in such an authoritative tone, it sounded as if she expected a disagreement. Her gaze locked into Maura's. "You'd be surprised how many women assume that just because their last paying job was in..." Ms. Hart paused, glanced at the resume, and looked up again. "Just because their last paying job was in 1960 they've nothing to offer."

Ms. Hart certainly held no brief for those who made such a foolish assumption and Maura was glad she was no longer in that group. Although it wasn't so many months ago, she had to admit to herself, when she too hadn't known that managing a house, balancing the family budget, raising children well, and entertaining a husband's clients were as real work as any paid labor. She nodded, feeling that this shared wisdom established a valuable equality.

"I was particularly interested in something on the house organ," she confided. She leaned forward, gesturing toward her papers, which included two photocopied sheets from the *Globe*. "As you can see, I did some publicity releases for the Coalition."

Ms. Hart promptly turned to the papers and skimmed them. "Mmmm," she said and smiled. "You've done some nice work here. I tell you what, we don't have any openings right away in this particular area, but why don't you let me keep this material and if something turns up, I'll let you know right away."

"Fine," Maura agreed. "However," she added quickly, "I was also interested in the training program." Even a few months ago Maura couldn't have made that transition. And although Ms. Hart explained that the program was really designed for younger people — "Not that you can call maturity being over the edge" — Maura nevertheless felt that she had introduced a new possibility smoothly and had not simply accepted a negative. She had been assertive while avoiding the mistake of being aggressive. Ms. Hart's explanation also made sense:

"Maturity implies experience — albeit life experience — and our training programs are really pitched toward those who don't have this. Thus they're going to be willing and satisfied with a starting position for a while." Ms. Hart looked at her openly as an equal, which Maura appreciated.

"Now people with some maturity," she continued, "just can't be satisfied with that sort of starting position, and they shouldn't be. In other words," Ms. Hart laughed, "I'm afraid your qualifications are just too good for us. But I'm going to keep you in mind." She closed the folder. "And you know," she added sincerely, "it's been a real pleasure." She extended her hand. "If there's one thing we really like to see, it's a woman going back into the market, showing that not only her formal education but her life experience is negotiable and profitable."

"Experience teaches," quipped Maura lightly with just the right shade of irony, and Ms. Hart laughed again.

"It's been a real pleasure," she said.

Although nothing concrete had been determined, Maura felt that the interview had been both encouraging and valuable and real communication had been established.

Maura's next interview was even less productive, but paradoxically it was even more exhilarating. She had selected Executive Placement from the yellow pages. It proved a good choice. The office, which was softly lit, conveyed a sense of spaciousness by the adroit placement of marbled mirrors and generous use of plants. The agent, a stout woman with stylish, football-shouldered suit and hair like whipped egg white, was cordial. Glancing quickly over the resume sheets, she rapped them against the desk to even the edges and pushed them crisply toward Maura.

"Editorial," she said decisively. "That's where you belong. Editorial."

She placed one elbow to either side of the desk blotter and leaned forward. "Look." Her voice sank to a conspiratorial level because, Maura guessed, she wasn't supposed to give out information to a person that wasn't officially a client. "You're a college graduate. You've done organizational work. You've done some writing. I'm not going to mislead you by keeping these papers. What we handle," she added drily, "is really secretarial positions." There was no denying that this was a disappointment. Suddenly Mrs. Baldwin snapped her fingers with a small explosion. Her eyes glinted. "Have you tried the education houses?"

Maura lowered her gaze. She liked Mrs. Baldwin, who had an efficient, no-nonsense attitude about her. True, she was the sort of woman whom George would have casually dismissed as "aggressive — a phony," but if she had listened a little less to George, she might be on the other side of the desk now. It was a delicate situation, however, for not only had she tried education houses, she had combed them. They had been her first thought.

"I tried a few," she admitted reluctantly. "I mean, you know, Hall, Addison-Wesley. . . ." To admit failure like that was painful and yet, gloriously, Mrs. Baldwin wasn't put off. Instead she said: "Idiots." Her voice was scathing. For an instant her gaze became abstracted, then came alive again with inspiration.

"New York. That's all there is to it. New York." She got up brusquely and came around the desk, picking up the resume folder and slapping it into Maura's hand as if it were a diploma. "Let me tell you this, my dear, you've got the stuff." She paused. "Do you have to stay in this town?" she asked kindly.

Maura rose slowly. "Not really," she said. "I'm separated."

"Then go to New York," said the woman heartily. "Don't sell yourself short." As they walked toward the door, Mrs. Baldwin touched Maura's arm gently. "You know, this is really your golden chance. I'll give you a piece of advice. Looking for a job isn't easy, but if you've got it, flaunt it." She paused again. "Look up some old classmates. They could have connections." Her blue eyes glittered so sympathetically that Maura couldn't tell her she couldn't do that. There were limits after all. Maybe after she got a job, then she could call.

At the doorway Mrs. Baldwin made a signal to the next applicant. As the girl rose, the agent gave Maura a wink. "Do me a favor," she said brightly. "Let me know when you land the big one, because you're going to."

As she rang for the elevator Maura found herself unaccountably smiling—Wouldn't that be something?—and quickly she stifled the image of herself that floated for just the shadow of an instant across her inner eye: Laura in understated black wool, an Albert Nipon probably, and a single strand of pearls. She and a young author were standing in front of a window from which the World Trade Center towers were just visible. Now that really is silly, she told herself.

The rain had stopped and the streets were drying as Maura stepped onto Boylston Street. A thin edge of sunlight had summoned the

210

homeless from their corners. They lay propped against stone abutments, sprawled on the library steps, monster rag dolls, abandoned by the children who'd gone away. Maura shivered. She looked at the pigeons, strutting at the edge of puddles. A construction worker, straddling a steel beam, was eating his lunch, and she thought about spring.

She thought about open windows and the pots of fresh daffodils and the French boy who'd been at MIT her senior year at Wellesley and who had taken her dancing at a party down by the lake, under the stars. Those had been magic days and she hadn't really thought about them for almost thirty years, as if even thinking of them would have been a betrayal of George, who had had to work so hard just to get a foothold.

In the spring the windows had been open in the dining hall and you could hear the thunk of tennis balls and the phones ringing from the floor above. Sometimes the calls had been for Maura and she would leave the dining hall walking casually, as if it didn't really matter, but aware all the time of the eyes following her, filled with curiosity and a touch of envy, because she had been popular.

For the first time in years she felt a surge of superiority. A puff of wind blew freshly against her face. Even if George hadn't left for the best of reasons, it was turning out for the best. Maybe it would be like a movie she had seen once: when they were both really established again and both remarried, then they would meet in some funny little out of the way place. . . .

Suddenly she remembered the Bird Cage at Lord & Taylor, where she'd always eaten when she had come in town for the children's clothes. She would treat herself to lunch there.

Pushing through the revolving glass doors away from the street and into the perfumed, glass-countered aisles, she stopped abruptly, struck by an unaccountable sense of rightness. Her eyes took in the brightly lighted displays of gold and silver jewelry, the alcoves where incredibly thin women moved decisively in front of racks of new springtime clothes, while still others circled slowly, arms cradling colored silks and linens, waiting for still something else to catch the eye. It was, Maura thought happily, like a secular church: nothing ever really changed in these stores. There was always the perfume, always the women in pink smocks hovering over their stoppered bottles, the little ovals of turquoise, aqua, and pearl eye shadow, the pots of feathery powders that "With just a touch. There. High on the cheekbone...brings out the real you."

But disappointingly, the Bird Cage had changed; it was now the American Cafe. Still that was all right, she thought, quelling an impulse toward nostalgia. It was good for things to change, and she wished she had, at least enough to dare a glass of wine alone at lunch. But she wasn't quite at that place yet.

Although she'd brought a P. D. James as a hedge against eating all by herself, Maura only pretended to read it. At the next table a mother and daughter wrangled over an upcoming party: "Mummy, I can't wear that...." the girl wailed. Maura shot the speaker a covert glance, wondering what the "that" was and if indeed it could possibly do any offense to such clear-skinned perfection. To her left was an even better conversation. A tall young woman, leaning almost onto her friend, whispered: "And do you know what he did to me?" Much to Maura's regret, the women left in a flurry of parcels before the story was told. Still, hearing even that much had been fun.

When she paid the bill, Maura took two instead of one after-dinner mints from the glass bowl next to the register. She nursed the crumbling little pink pillows of mint on her tongue all the way down the escalator and back through the revolving doors to the street.

Maura sat on the stiff leather couch in the reception room of the office of Pierce-Martin, thumbing through a year old copy of *Time* and regretting that she no longer smoked. She would take it up again as there was no one now to hang it over her head that she was deliberately courting cancer. Although her appointment had been for one o'clock, it was already quarter to two and Mr. Pierce, with whom she had the appointment, had not yet returned.

"I'm really sorry," said the receptionist at one-thirty. She was a sweet-faced young girl with a moussed halo of blond hair. She was working on a blackhead at the corner of her nose. "There." She snapped the compact closed, patted the raw spot with a tissue, and looked at her watch. "Would you like to come back tomorrow perhaps? We've had a hideously busy day. We're just behind in everything."

Maura shook her head. "Don't worry about it," she said kindly. "I know how these things can be." But the fact was that although she had reassured the girl, she was now beginning to worry. The receptionist was typing and didn't look up again. Maura regretted being quite so accommodating; it would be hard to reintroduce the subject of not waiting. Just as she was getting too nervous, the hall door opened and a middle-aged man in an overcoat came in. "Hi," he said to the receptionist and disappeared into the back. In ten minutes the buzzer on the desk sounded, and the girl, picking up a pad, went into the back also.

Without the typing, the room became deafeningly still. Maura began to feel shaky as if the pale, color-coordinated walls and carpets were closing in. She fought it off, counting the glossy leaves on the dracaena in the corner.

The girl had reappeared. "Mr. Pierce can see you now." She ushered Maura down carpeted space to a paneled door, which she thrust open. "Here," she announced, as if Maura weren't so much a person as a package.

Maura peered around self-consciously. Shelves ran from floor to ceiling around the room. They were crammed with the company's publications, sports trophies, and several framed photographs. In one an attractive blond woman in white jeans waved from the deck of a sailboat; in another the same woman in a bikini chased two blond youngsters across a stretch of sand; in still another—an older, more formal black-and-white portrait—the woman sat with hands folded on her lap, looking outward, her hair lit from behind to create a sort of halo. Against that frame leaned a candid shot showing the woman, two teenage boys, and a man in a T-shirt. The figures in the photo had their arms draped over each others' shoulders. They were grinning into the camera from a backdrop of blue sky and sails.

The man in the T-shirt was a slightly younger edition of the one who sat at the desk in the center of the room. His arms were linked now behind his head in a gesture of open informality, but he had the same thick confident grin, the genial air of someone equally at home and successful among books as sailboats.

"It's good to see you, Maura," he said amiably. "I'm terribly sorry you had to wait." One elbow tilted toward a chair. "You know how it is. When you get behind on things, you never seem to catch up."

Maura sat down. "Yes. Isn't it awful." She hoped that didn't sound too presumptuous, as if she thought they shared the same obligations, but it always took her a bit off stride to be called promptly by her first name.

Mr. Pierce, finally unlinking his hands and leaning forward, didn't seem to notice. He was fumbling with the cellophane string on a pack of cigarettes. Pulling the string loose, he crumpled the cellophane, opened the silver foil with his thumb, and extended the pack toward her. "Cigarette?"

She shook her head. "I gave them up two years ago."

He grinned. "Ah, some people have all the will power." He took one himself, lit it, and drew in a deep breath of smoke. "Well now," he said, nodding toward the folder open on his desk. "I see here you went to Wellesley. Now that's my place. Unofficial alumnus. My wife's a Wellesley girl, you know."

"Is she?" said Maura gaily. "Isn't it a small world. Tell me. What's her maiden name? Maybe we can play 'do you know'."

Mr. Pierce laughed as if she had said something witty. Then he shook his head, leaning back again. "I don't think so," he said heartily. "She's quite a bit younger than we are. Class of '67, you know."

Although she was disposed to like this man, Maura couldn't help but find his remark rude. There was no way he could tell when she'd graduated. The resume advisor had told her not to put in dates. Granted, she had noted that her last full-time employment was in the early sixties, but still he had no right to assume when she'd graduated.

"Well now," Mr. Pierce was saying, steepling his fingers and leaning forward on the point to regard her solemnly. "Well now, what can I do for you today?"

Maura swallowed. "Well, as I said in my letter, I was looking for something in editing." For the shadow of a second a mask of perplexity shadowed Mr. Pierce's blue eyes. Then he patted his hair and smiled encouragingly. "Of course," he said. "You were the one who answered

214

the ad in the *Globe*. He picked up her papers and skimmed them quickly. "You're interested in doing editing and have written some press releases." He looked at her for affirmation.

"That's right," she prodded. "And your office did call."

"Mmmm." He was glancing through her papers again. "Mmmmm. Mmmm. Well, I don't think we have anything quite in your line...." He said it not at all unkindly but as if it were quite an inconsequential remark. "I mean," he went on, "we did want a reader, and I can see why we got in touch with you—you've got nice qualifications—but we are a technical house, and we do handle a great deal of material that has a scientific orientation."

"But..." Maura found herself blushing hotly, "your office...nothing was said about science in the ad." She felt bewildered.

"Right," said Mr. Pierce blandly. "We really should have." He looked at her cheerfully. "You aren't into programming, are you?"

Unexpectedly, a lump swelled in her throat and she found it hard to breathe. She mustn't panic. The job wasn't gone, not yet. It couldn't be.

"I'm not exactly an expert," she laughed lightly. "But my son was into computers in high school and I did pick up quite a bit of basic knowledge."

Mr. Pierce looked jovial. "Exactly," he said. "Didn't you feel as if you got a whole new education with the kids in school." He ducked his head in the direction of the boys grinning in front of the sailboats. "God, we didn't have in college the sort of stuff they're teaching them now in high school. Why, I said to Brad when I saw the kind of Physics they were giving him, 'God, it's a good thing your old man got out of here before they had all this stuff or you'd be the son of a gas station attendant'." He laughed explosively. "I mean, can you imagine, having to make it now? And the computers. They just take all that for granted. I've bought myself a Mac, though. User friendly, you know." He was closing her folder, smiling across at her. "But that's not quite enough, is it?" His voice had grown serious. "Look, I am sorry if we got you here on a wild goose chase. I didn't put the ad in the paper. My girl did." He grinned. "Another youngster. She just took it for granted that anyone who'd answer would, well you know, be her generation. Know all that computer sort of stuff."

He was pushing the papers back at her, dismissing her. Then something perfectly terrible happened. Maura's voice became disconnected from her will, and to her horror she heard it declaring that she intended to learn all about computering and programming and software and all that, and that she was actually enrolling in a technical course and—worst of all—she was saying with a silly, modest little laugh that she always learned everything so quickly and that there really was no problem. She could see the amiable look fading from Mr. Pierce's blue eyes and—oh, she didn't blame him—distaste replacing it.

"I don't see much point in doing all that," he was saying coldly, but her dreadful voice kept going, actually whining as he started to get up. He was beginning to hate her because she was forcing him to be rude, forcing him to say: "You're too old. We don't want you. You haven't any real experience." But blessedly, the voice stopped as abruptly as it had begun. Blessedly, she heard herself say, as if all the rest had been a joke, "Well, of course, I don't really think that this position would be quite what I'm comfortable in, but you have to try everything."

Relief flooded Mr. Pierce's wary features. And now, she too was standing, laughing almost flirtatiously. "But I do think your operation sounds just fantastic," she was saying. Had he even told her about what he did publish? She couldn't remember, but it didn't matter as he was smiling again. "And I do hope you find the right person, but you know us liberal arts people." Her voice was perfectly arch.

"Precisely," he said and then added something disparaging about computer types. He ushered her to the door with genuine gallantry. "As I always say, I feel like a Wellesley girl myself. Well, not quite. But at least you girls don't have to worry. You'll always turn up something, even if it's just an old codger like myself." Then together they commiserated about those who really had no training at all. So sad.

And there now, she thought, going down in the elevator, tired like an exhausted runner. What a narrow escape she had had. But it had all turned out all right in the long run. She shivered at the memory of how she had almost acted, in fact, had acted—there's nothing to be gained by not being honest with yourself. But she had retrieved herself—you must remember your good points.

216

Even though Pierce-Martin had been her last planned appointment, it was only three, plenty of time to make one or two other applications. Maura walked over to Federal Street and up Franklin to Filene's department store. The sidewalk was glazed with a thin rain and she tied on a plastic rain hat, although ordinarily she found them ugly and didn't like to wear them. Still one must be practical. At Filene's she made an application for a temporary salesperson, but the women behind the counter said they only hired college students for temporary positions, so she changed that to full time and then went straight to Jordan's where she filled out the full-time application form.

All in all it had been a very busy day. Catching the four-thirty bus, Maura found herself too tired to even look through the classifieds, although she had automatically bought the paper at the bus kiosk. She did, she thought, deserve a little holiday, so she read *Death of a Nightingale*, rereading the two pages she had merely skimmed at the Cafe. When the bus stopped she was already well into Dalgliesh's speculation about the second murder. How funny it was that she could remember bits and pieces of the puzzle because, of course, she had read all of P. D. James before, but who did what or why never seemed to stick in her mind.

A peck of cold stung against her cheek as she walked back from the bus, and she realized that out here in the suburbs the rain had long ago turned to snow. Already the lawns were lacy white. At the house, which was quite large now that she was living alone, she took off her interview clothes and changed into woolly slacks and slippers.

There was just enough time before Dan Rather to broil a piece of chicken. Popping it into the oven and pouring herself a small drink, she went back into the living room to finish her chapter. It hadn't, after all, been a bad day. There was no point in kidding herself that the Pierce-Martin interview hadn't been a disappointment, but she had never really liked that sort of person—the bluff, hearty type. And the woman at Hancock had been quite cordial as had the woman at Executive Placement. Then she remembered the boy on the bus and smiled. He must have found her attractive. And there were Filene's or Jordan's.

Either one would be a perfectly adequate stopgap.

Maura finished her chapter and the next two before the kitchen timer rang. As she went out to the kitchen to fix her plate, she turned on the TV to warm up. For some reason the chicken no longer appealed. She wrapped it and put it in the fridge. In its place she arranged a small salad of cottage cheese on a canned half peach.

Photo by Sandy Thacker

Architect
Holly Hildebrand

She drew the dimensions, but did not set the bounds.
Her rooms were white lines on blue papers:
some days she saw in them lovers, other days, dying men.
She would have liked to have painted them,
a Van Gogh violet for the master bedroom,
Matisse yellow for the kitchen, a *trompe l'oeil*
in the dining room to disorient the guests.
To the powder room, she would send flocks
of paper nightingales, lavender, silent for now,
but ready to tell all later: the songs sung
between the satin sheets, the coos that came
with conceptions, the promises that ran,
like a prodigy's black ink, down her walls,
always white-lined on blue paper.

Therapist

Ruth Harriet Jacobs

To Margaret E. Gordon

It had to be a garden in the wood.
You did not choose the easy packaged seed
but moved wild plants according to their need
encouraged each to grow the way it should
around the rocks and trees as best it could.
You freed the soil so that the plants could feed
but worked with patience, never to impede
the natural patterns each had found so good.

So too, you take each of us, as we are
all covered with the choking, rampant blight
of fantasy and guilt and hates that mar
each breath we draw, each timid hope we fight
and waiting, skillful, planting here and there,
you feed us, free us, give us growing air.

Carol

Carol Barrett

Since we may never meet again
let us say how our lives have changed.
                                    — Anita Skeen

They called you my patient.
I called you my own name
and in that first hour of change
took your hand. They called me
unprofessional. It was not right
to move so fast. Touch is forbidden:
wait for the proper moment
when the patient is ready.
Clad in the arms of men
you had been waiting years.

          I changed
your chart, rewrote medical opinion.
This was worse: county records
are private property. They discussed us
at long tables, analyzed my error
in rooms without sunlight,
their pointed words whittling
the air like chopsticks.
They were certain you would never
trust one of them again. You waited.

They hoped
I had gotten sufficient supervision,
instructed the cotherapist to take
charge. He began by asking your name,
place of birth, the length of your mother's
labor, sexual identity. You gave him
my name, all that was important.
The others waited for their turns,
eyes vibrating the ashtrays. "Now what
is your problem?" he advanced. Our name
hit the one-way mirror like rivets.

He was commended for doing better.
They did not name us once,
scheduled you for individual treatment
with the primary supervisor.
He would handle the case well.

Before he was ready you left
for a new job. They insisted
this was moving too fast.
I celebrated alone. The cotherapist
was doing quite well now.
In the final hour our name holds
the chairs in place. A new intern
is assigned to write
our discharge summary.

On Becoming a Social Worker

Janet Carncross Chandler

My parents hoped I'd be a doctor —
in those days an improbable star.

I scornfully rejected teaching (their profession).
My sister pre-empted my becoming a librarian.

A tendency to forget whole passages
in violin recitals convinced my parents

I was not right for music making, leaving
my own choices, nursing or social work.

When I presented myself at the school for nursing,
I assured the director I would not need the dorm

as I was getting married. "Then, young lady,
you'll not be a nurse." "Well, at least," said my mother,

"you won't be carrying bed pans." And so,
delivering Sunday dinners to an elderly churchmember

was to be the beginning of thirty years spent in trying
to help others meet their needs. Social work professors

would later teach not to "do for" but to help
clients learn to help themselves.

I still think my mother's tenderly succulent chicken,
famous blueberry muffins and angel food cake

along with my hug and kiss on her soft cheek
probably did my elderly isolate a lot of good.

Graduate school seemed a succession of small blows
and little triumphs, as I learned to listen creatively,

to resist the impulse to impress my values on others.
Gradually, I learned to relate warmly

without smothering, donned the hood of professional social worker,
moved up from child welfare to medical social worker

then to the heights: Psychiatric Social Worker, complete
with the snobbery of one who discovers too late

she could have been a pyschologist, even a psychiatrist.
A young man would have learned in time to switch.

How could the years slip by without my noticing?
Gone was the notion of "do-gooder," of being a catalyst

without becoming involved. A new freedom when
as group therapist, I was expected to react, interact,

at times confront a client. Strange to learn so late
that families are important, and family members

working together can untie knotty problems
untouched by individual therapy.

Along with my patients, I began to expand and grow.
Better late, you know.

Mother Teresa in Calcutta

Savina A. Roxas

Wins a gold medal
at 69, descending
the dark slopes of Bengali
gleaning the dying,
the orphaned, the unwanted
taking them away
from the gutters,
the rats, the Palace
of Death, to her lair
for the living. She

feeds them, wiping their faces
clean, breathes her warmth
into them, the dust of her
smarting the eyes of those
who look the other way.
Her curved body rocks
that rotting city
with beds and clean white
sheets for the throwaways
while they wait to leave
one body for another.
Easing their passage
through the tunnel.
She is the midwife:

Agnes Gonxha Bojaxhiu
five feet tall, Yugoslav,
candles for eyes, from
southwest of Sarajevo
where Olympics were held.

Photo by Lori Burkhalter-Lackey

Vital Signs
Susan Jacobson

PULSE

Say, "Good morning, I need your vital signs."
Pop a probe under the tongue
(or in the armpit, if the jaws are wired)
of a meekly opened mouth.
Reach for the satin skin of the inner wrist,
(or behind the knee cap, if the arms are broken)
(or the carotid, if both arms and legs are broken)
your fingers ignoring the soft swell of veins,
finding, pressing the radial artery,
waiting for the deep throb of rhythmic tides
one, two, three...for ten seconds...
9 times 6 is 54, 17 makes 102 ...

Say, "Welcome to Agony General
where we organize your misery for you.
Please remember that sleeping is not allowed
and anyone caught sleeping
will be awakened immediately.
Our new physical therapist has issued orders
for everyone to jog down to the Allegheny
for a nice brisk swim before breakfast."

Photo by Rhonda Oxley

TEMPERATURE

Wait for the beep-beep of the probe to go off.
Remove it from the patient's mouth (or wherever).
Remove the cover. Make an impossible
under-the-table-banked-off-the-wall
shot into the trash basket.
Award yourself 9.5 for degree of difficulty.
37° celsius is normal, 37.5° a febrility,
38° serious business, 34° probably death,
(or the patient has been drinking ice water).
Remind the patient to breathe deeply
and to cough "hawkers." Raise an eyebrow
at the clutter on the bedside table, and say,
"I see you've gotten someone to smuggle
real food in here. Don't get caught,"
then clean up the mess.

Listen to the patient complain
about the food, the noise, the silence,
the nurses, the doctors, housekeeping,
the heating/cooling system, the bed, etc.
Tell him the purpose of a hospital
is to make you so miserable that you go home,
and that this hospital is the best in the city.

RESPIRATIONS

Count the number of times the chest or abdomen
rises and falls: do not let the patient catch you:
if he knows what you're doing his breathing will alter,
if she doesn't, she'll think you're a pervert.
Note the particular odor of sweat and breath,
normal early-morning lousy, like horses in August,
or perk-induced, or fevered and tinged with bacteria.
Run a practiced eye over the body, noting
the tenting of Hoffmans under the sheet.
If the patient has a broken pelvis and leg (or legs),
tell him, "The volleyball game against pediatrics
is scheduled for 9 am and I want you out in the hall
for calisthenics at 8:30. We're not having any more
humiliating defeats by a bunch of brats in wheelchairs."
Pick the heaviest set nurse on the shift and tell
the patient you're using her for the volleyball:
"So we'll have an edge. We'll murder them."

Listen to the patient get all over his/her case
for: falling off a ladder/roof/chair/porch,
cutting off his toes with a lawn mower,
slicing off his/her fingers with a radial arm saw
or an Isaly's meat slicer or an electric miter box, etc.,
driving drunk, driving sober but fiddling with the radio.
(Remember it is human nature to blame things on people;
the nice ones blame themselves, the nasty ones blame you.)
Say, "Welcome to the human race, a world-wide community
of spaz-offs, klutzes, do-dos and dumkopfs.
Self-pity is permitted here on Thursday mornings
from 1 am until 3 am, and self-hatred is scheduled
on Monday mornings between 12 and 12:01 am."

BOWEL MOVEMENTS

Ask the patient if he/she has had a bowel movement.
Listen to a detailed description of just how much,
and when and what quality/quantity, and texture —
not to mention degree of satisfaction — or
note the need for milk of mag, suppository, enema or
dynamite. Tell him/her that "Ellen's favorite method
is to hang you by the ears from the IV standard
with your butt one inch from the pan — after visiting
hours and all night or until gravity does its work,"
whereas, "I prefer just to jump off the overhead bar
onto the abdomen. It's a lot quicker."
One can never just get vitals: as soon as you walk
in the room, they want something. First, empty
the urinal or ask if they prefer a bedpan to a walker.
(They will, of course, pick whichever is hardest for you.)

BLOOD PRESSURE

If both arms are broken, bruised or dislocated,
put the cuff around the thigh and listen behind the knee.
If both arms and legs are in Hoffmans, casts, splints,
etc., try a radial pressure, with cuff on forearm,
or a pedal pulse with cuff on calf. If none of the above
is available, do not guess (although this is possible
and, with practice, fairly accurate derived from
the complex relationship of pulse and temperament,
plus/minus pain, imminence of surgery and whether
the patient has had a fight with his wife, or
her husband, or a night nurse, resident or you).
Under no circumstances use the carotid artery.

Listen always,
wait, always,
for *the* vital sign.
Not the chuckle, or snort or guffaw or howl
in response to your nonsense:
that only indicates they're alive.

Wait for the day Randy says—
weeks into dressing changes on his stump,
and the mangled mess that is/was the other foot,
weeks of worry over how his little girl
is going to react to his disfigurement/crippling,
of how his wife *is* reacting to it,
of clutching a football a Steeler has brought him,
of biting towels, wringing your hands, weeping—
wait for the day Randy says,
"I'm going to save 50% on socks."

Glance at Ellen and see
your tears in her eyes.
Hear her ask, "So?
You're not going to wear
a sock on your prosthesis?
That's tacky,"
and Randy's response: "Sure, I am,
but I'm only going to sweat on one foot
so I'll just switch socks the next day."
Laugh or chuckle or step into the hall and cry:
this patient is going to live.

Photo by Sandra Gregory

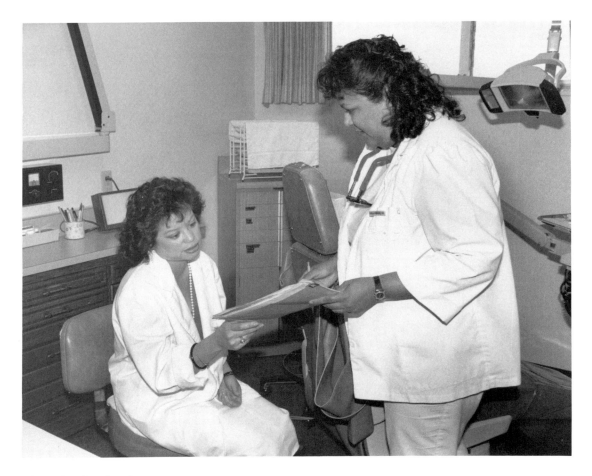

Photo by Sandra Gregory

The Mother-in-Law Diaries

Elaine Starkman

JUNE 2

Woke hopeful and energetic. Must be from reading May Sarton last night. I'd been depressed thinking about the uselessness of Ma's life and all our techniques for prolonging life when the quality of living remains mimimal. But who am I to say? This morning — voilà — there's Ma chewing gum and humming a beautiful Yiddish melody.

We worked in the house: I found some potatoes. She's happily peeling them for a *kugel*. So here I am, I, who for years have tried to escape the kitchen, am back in it.

JUNE 13

Ma watching daytime TV with the kids. Lillian Hellman talking about her life. Told Ma she was a famous writer.

"So what does she have? A husband, children, a home?"

If Ma knew that writing keeps me alive and sane, what would she say?

Told the kids to go easy on daytime TV. Not about to start the summer with that thing blaring all day long.

Amy protests. "But it's good for Grandma; it gives her something to do. Otherwise, she gets bored and picks her head."

"Too bad. Grandma's not going to sit in front of the boob tube all day long in my house."

JULY 21

Do my neighbors really think Ma's "great help around the house?" Maybe some women her age are, but I'm beginning to learn she doesn't want to cook.

"I forgot how. I cooked all my life," she says. And here I've been knocking myself out to get her to cook, to feel useful. Am I taking this too seriously? Am I trying too hard to emulate Ma's dedication to the family, her goodness, knowing *I can never live up to either?*

JULY 26, ASHLAND, OREGON

My reactions vary from what a burden to admiration. In and out of the car, shoes on, shoes off, the dry heat keeping in all the odors. Not one complaint; she's holding up marvelously.

Round one: Amy refuses to sleep in the same bed with Ma. Maury's furious. Ma's hurt. I take my child's view—we brought our children up to be selfish; we can't expect them to accommodate now. I tell Amy to sleep outside in a sleeping bag. She does. Maury fumes. I feel like killing him.

We're taking Ma to the Shakespeare Festival. Won't the family think well of us? Send them all cards; show them.

Amy: "Why didn't we hire someone to watch Grandma at home? Why can't we be like a normal American family—without a Grandma?"

Because we're not like other families. *Because what appears normal is not normal.*

JULY 27

Ma picks berries, a familiarity from her childhood. She's ecstatic. Again, in and out of the car, to the toilet, to the gift shop, the shoes again; no, we can't take a boat ride on Crater Lake—it's too much for Grandma. Where's a chair for her? She's exhausted.

Ma, are you sorry you came? No, no better I come. How many more years to come?

Maury gives her his white cap; instant transformation. No more Eastern European *Babushka*, but a sporty West Coast Granny. All she needs is a pair of slacks. No, no, she laughs. She's not going to have her *tuches* hanging out.

We stop to eat. "My treat, from my money. Take it from my account, Maury."

At the cabin she falls into bed but is up in half an hour. Maury watches her like a hawk.

"Are you upset we didn't go on the boat ride?"

"It doesn't matter," I lie.

238

JANUARY 14

My friends were right; I didn't understand what was in store when Ma came to live here. I didn't define limits. I understand now that *I* needed to have her. I needed to be the good one, *to play that role, as much as I deny it in myself.* I had to show others I'm "better" than they; as much as I deny that the Certificate of Appreciation for driving seniors matters to me, I do need that kind of recognition. Never thought I did; only thought I needed recognition from my teaching and writing.

FEBRUARY 5

What is there about a simple sneeze that sends Ma into such laughter? Some old-country superstition connected with it? Her response made Amy silly. She wanted Ma to dance with her. First time in a long while Ma's laughed.

Later she actually got up and volunteered to help me clean the chickens. Saw her grab some of the skins I was cooking and put them in the pocket of her apron and walk out of the room to eat them. Then she came back into the kitchen shamefacedly, smacked her lips, and said, "I got everything I need."

FEBRUARY 24

Read in the *Oakland Tribune* about an eighty-one-year-old woman who died from a mugging. Sick society we live in. Sick, and I, too, am part of the sickness. Didn't give Ma her lunch until after two today. Finally I called her. "Are you hungry, Ma?"

"Yes, I'm very hungry."

"Why didn't you tell me? I could have made lunch sooner."

"You were busy at your desk."

Not to eat when you're hungry; to have to wait until your daughter—in-law is ready to feed you. Sick.

MARCH 27

Passover was early this year. I grumbled through all the work. We had seventeen people. Ma was excited by the crowd. Maury came home early and helped Ma get ready. Jon's girlfriend was surprised. "Is Jon going to do that for you when you get old?" she laughed.

We put a candle on the Passover cake and sang "Happy Birthday" to Ma as her birthday is around this time. Think she's eighty-two; Maury says she lied on her passport.

So I was the good dutiful daughter praised by guests, all the while in the back of my head wishing I'd gone on the disarmament mission to the U.N. with a woman artist I met last week. That would have been some Passover! Activists never seem to have any family to cope with. They've broken with family demands a long time ago.

APRIL 10
Admit it. It's better when someone's here to take care of Ma, better for her as well as for me. How listless Ma was yesterday without Cedora, and I was too busy to talk with her the way Cedora does. Felt so bad for her I went out and bought her herring and sour cream. She just sat in her chair the entire day. When a neighbor came in for a moment, Ma didn't acknowledge her presence.

Although I managed to be quite productive despite being alone with her, I somehow felt dehumanized—like one of those high-achieving women who accomplishes her goal by caring nothing for others.

APRIL 11
How quietly she rests in her chair waiting for Cedora to come. What trust and faith in others. If only I could rest like that. But today I feel like a prisoner in my own house. All my responsibility usurped. Blessed be old black women who care for old white women, who change their sheets and do not hate them, who accept their age and do not fear it.

Am I jealous of Cedora, too? Of her ability to work with Ma and not to hate it? That she can sit outside in the yard with Ma in peace while I pace about inside? Today I am a prisoner....I cannot rest.

APRIL 24
Seven-forty. Maury at work, Amy at school; the two of us together. She's up now. I hear her. She's sitting up in bed staring blankly at the wall. How does she feel when she wakes up to another day of nothingness? Her room smells like a nursing home. Her hair disheveled,

240

her glasses on. Did she sleep with them on all night? Shall I dash in and take her out of bed. No, I have to wake myself before I'm ready to confront her. Let her try for herself. She's not aware of me or what I'm doing. Concerned with her not feeling well. Shall I go in and put drops in her eyes or wait for Toni to do it; she'll be here by ten; then she can take care of Ma.

She's coming out now, and I'm not ready for her. Smile, encourage her. "Good morning, Ma. Are you ready to eat your breakfast?"

"Not now, darling, I'm too dizzy. Is that girl coming today to help me?"

"Toni's coming. Cedora will be back next week."

"The young one who talks too much?"

"I thought she kept you company, Ma. I thought you liked to watch 'I Love Lucy' with her."

Silence. So be it. As soon as Toni comes, off to my room to write until noon, the sounds of voices drifting through my door. Then at six Maury will add his overly-patient sounds. "And how's the dizzy Mamma today?"

"Much better, Mauryle, much better."

JUNE 1

She's shitting all over herself. Is it because she knows the truth: that I'm planning to send her back to her daughter this summer. Toni's fussing so, that it's easier for me to clean up the mess myself. Both bathrooms. Clean up the shit. I should be used to it from the kids. Yes, Maury. Ma's an old powerless woman who can't even control her bowels today. How that powerlessness manifests itself in our lives!

Amy comes into the bathroom and watches me. "Get out of here!" I shout, not wanting her to see.

"Boy, you're a crab! No wonder Dad would rather talk to Grandma at dinner. She always smiles and listens to him."

"Yeah?" I yell from the bathroom floor. "I wish Grandma would croak!"

"Mom! You're really awful!"

God, the words just slipped out of me, the way the shit just slipped out of Ma.

School Bus

Randeane Tetu

During the summer of her fifty-second year, Janice Colby came back from the large empty place caused by the death of her husband Benny to the small things—birds racketing in the summer trees, the sound of the teakettle whistle, and the note from unemployment that since she had shown no effort to procure another job, her unemployment benefits were being terminated. Any questions, call Mandy.

Janice poured the screaming water over her tea bag in the blue willow cup and turned over the form note. The perforations where the printout paper had been torn on all edges were more noticeable on the back because it was blank.

Janice never made any attempt to look for work in the summer because when school started in September she put on the cowboy hat from her closet shelf and drove bus number 7 through the nine months until June. Then she collected unemployment because during the summer months there was no call for someone to drive school bus.

Before she sat down at the table with her tea, Janice thought she might walk to the closet and get the hat from the shelf and put it on, but then she sat down and, instead, watched the black shadows the sweet peas made across the back steps.

She turned the note back to the printed side. "Look at this," she said to Benny. "Look at this." She was sure Benny leaned over the edge of the firmament to look at her when she needed him or when she'd accomplished something on her own—but not when she held his pillow in a tight knot and rubbed herself against it.

She thought about Benny in a way similar to the way she thought about mirrors. When her makeup looked nice and she batted her eyelashes twice, she was sure that there was a world behind mirrors looking in on this one. But when she grimaced to floss her teeth, she hoped there wasn't.

"Look at this."

242

She listened for his voice to say, "If you like driving school bus, do it, and stop doing it if you don't," which is what he told her every June when she said, "Maybe I'll get another job."

Janice liked the smell of the bus. She liked climbing up the ridged steps and sweeping out the clutter of dirt and candy wrappers and spitballs, barrettes, wads of dittoed paper.

She drove the bus and watched the driveways where they met the road looking for book bags and lunch boxes and things left behind. When the bus was empty, she watched the driveways for whose car was going to work. In cold weather the exhausts of cars batted the tar. She watched for the dogs that were tied up and could get into the garage where the door was slightly above the sill and for the dogs that were loose. She watched for the mailman's small four-wheeled box that she met between Decker's and the stop sign.

After they parked the buses, the bus drivers took over the coffee shop for breakfast. Then Janice had time until the afternoon run. At the end of each June she thought, "I don't know. Maybe I should get a real job."

When she thought of jobs, she pictured the posters she'd seen as a child in the war years, pictures of women with their sleeves rolled above their muscles, women holding hammers and soldering guns and smiling in their men's work clothes.

Janice watched the shadows of the sweet peas fall onto the hot back steps.

Maybe they were right at the unemployment office. Maybe she needed a job this year to fill the space from breakfast until afternoon. She washed and set away the blue willow cup and saucer. She called Mandy at the unemployment office and had Mandy tell her they were "cracking down," "getting tough," and she would have to show proof of interviews. Mandy gave her the number at the bank where they were looking for clerical help—she couldn't type, they would disqualify her—and of the train depot where they were looking for a waitress—she wasn't quick on her feet. They would say she was too old.

Janice made the appointments back-to-back and dressed in the grey suit she had worn at Benny's funeral. She batted her eyelashes in the mirror.

The bank wanted her without typing skills and the train depot needed her even if she couldn't run. "Young people," they told her, "don't want to work."

"I'll take the bank," she told Mandy on the phone, "because of the lighting and the counters and the smell of dried flowers and the hush of walking across the carpet." She set the teakettle on to boil.

She pulled the cowboy hat off the closet shelf and put it on above the suit. "Look at me," she grinned to Benny in the mirror.

Photo by Lori Burkhalter-Lackey

About Cleaning Bathrooms

Kathryn Eberly

It seems I'm always barging in
on somebody who's caught in a
compromising position. Right off,
they accuse me of spying.
What can I say?
How can I deny it?
I reply, muttering something
foolish about having to polish
the white porcelain or lay out
a fresh supply of paper towels.
But the embarrassed eyes follow me
out the squeaking black door,
they don't believe me.
For god's sake, why should I care
about the size of his dick or
whether or not she's been sitting
on the pot reading *Vogue* for
twenty minutes or who hurriedly
shoved a *Playboy* behind the stall?
And why would I take note of the
men who spray themselves with
cologne or the woman who plugs up
the john with tampons every single
month? No, it's pretty dull stuff.
But still they accuse me.
You Don't Look Like A Janitor.

Photo by Sandy Thacker

The words accost me,
I ignore them.
I lay the toilet paper out gingerly.
I spray the air with just the right
amount of deodorizer, I whistle a lot.
As far as I'm concerned if you've seen
one ass, you've seen them all.

Photo by Clytia Fuller

Photo by Marianne Gontarz

Mowing at Dusk

Barbara Crooker

Grass pours from the mower's side,
glitters in the last light.
There's satisfaction
in small tasks,
drifting in neutral,
the turf reduced
to simple geometry,
the blade cutting
a clean path,
a swath of green,
patterns of surf.
I could drown in this noise
that pours over me;
I glitter in the last light.
Scents of rose and tarragon
hang starry in the night air
where the catcher brushes them.
Fireflies wink on and on,
signals from the shore.
Landlocked in Pennsylvania,
my kitchen light beacons.
I rudder home in the salty dark.

Working in the Garden
Elizabeth Gilliland

I crosshatch the shadow of bud
beneath the backlit petal, the rose
I recompose in the rose garden

where morning sun lights
all the roses living and dying—
variations on the theme of coral.

Sweet alyssum placed by a woman
between the thorny stems...
There cannot be enough of musing

on these roses, the broken walk
crossing between quadrants of earth
that gives off rich smells after rain,

and quiescence of unnameable music;
seen growth and color in a rhythm
where what is arranged, growing

and dying has been arranged for retreat
from the larger world of cities and cars.

Finally

Dori Appel

She's free now, no more
crazy mother to take care of
and no more whiny kids and no more
husband wheezing ever more slowly
over twenty years. She's free
to read the Sunday *Times*
with no one interrupting, to leave
her bed at night solely for her own
bladder's sake, to learn Italian,
plan a trip, buy marmalade
for her solitary toast.

Photo by Lori Burkhalter-Lackey

Breaking Formation
Elisavietta Ritchie

The aging artist packs
greyed silver, tattered towels,
chipped plates, a crusted palette,

shoe boxes marked Blown Fuses,
Zippers, Shade Pulls,
Sheep Skulls, Arrowheads.

Neighbors mothball, roll the rugs,
pile split mattresses, sprung chairs.
The mice within resettling,

all is stored in two back rooms
as if she were just off
to Florence until spring.

Muslin shrouds her canvases
stacked for cut-rate galleries.
Paints dried to stone are thrown away.

Bags for Charity; button shoes,
silk dresses, splattered smocks—
someone might find a use.

Still time before the van arrives
to hobble past her untilled fields,
barns where she hid out to paint,

the beach where cove and sea collide
beneath the lighthouse on the bluff.
Around a broken skiff the mallards wait

to gulp her scattered crusts.
Erect between her canes, she checks
the farm one final time, dry-eyed

until nine whistling swans
coo and flute low overhead,
fracture the sun in a broken formation.

Two Grey Hills

Nancy Roxbury Knutson

Sky of boundless blue
burnt red hillocks
scanty bush and dried bed,
a figure in full skirt
shawl over her head,
walking stick and dog.
This is where it begins
a Navajo herding her sheep.

Cloth binding his front legs
a tethered sorrel
hobbles out of cold morning
shadow behind the butte.
Toward winter feeding grounds
she walks on, skirting patches
of new snow glinting
in the new sun.

In spring she snips the fleece
from the flock. From shoulder,
flank, back, the longest wool.
She will not sell this year
to Fred Harvey traders or Shiprock
or auction at Crown Point.

Card it smooth. Dark and white
carded together for the tan,
grey of the hills.
Disc against thigh
she spins the spindle stick
till the wool is tight, fine,
seven or nine times.

When the sun sleeps a little longer,
no longer pounds the land so hard
she begins pushing the shed,
pulling the heddle. An intricate
pattern: Two Grey Hills.
As if from memory it grows
from the floor rising
higher than her reach.
Slacken the tension, lower
the weaving to its waist;
make the threads rise in reverse.
Loosen beam cords.
Rebuild the loom, string
warp four hands
and do it all again.

No storm pattern, Wide Ruin.
Daughters can weave rough,
cowboys, Chevys, American flag
with trading post dyes.
This will be a *biil*, dress
sewn of two weavings
with fine edges and feel.
For ceremony.
Comb and batten,
she beats the weft down.

Time to pass the sheep
to her daughters.
Perhaps pickups and school
are a good thing.
Her brown hands pull
the thread straight.
Through the hogan door
she notices the light
turn on the lava
and sandstone cliffs.
By first snow she will finish.

Working the Clay

Elisavietta Ritchie

She is demonstrating an ancient way to make pots. She needs no wheel, but places damp clay on a platform of stone.

The sun bursts between boulders: already the morning is warm. The pine which long gave her shade has now died.

She has worked here seventy years. She is rib-thin and wrinkled, her braids are grey. The mass of clay is heavy. With crimped fingers she flattens the base and we see that the pot will be large.

A man, also the color of clay, brings pails of water and more clay. She does not seem to notice. He chops the pine into logs. Others approach, to fill in the circle.

An eagle rises to split the hot sky.

She gropes for clay, rolls it into a snake, encircling the base with its gritty flesh. More snakes blend as she smoothes them, coil higher and higher, walling the base.

The sun is beginning to singe. She alone does not sweat. Still, it takes time, she works slowly. The man offers water. She shakes her head. The others wander away to the shade.

She fills her pipe with peculiar leaves, lights them and draws bitter smoke.

The lower wall is already firm. She adds ever more coils. The pot swells its circular belly. She seems tired, but continues to knead the clay into snakes into walls.

She can no longer reach. The man lifts her small body up toward the sun, lowers it gently into the pot.

He stands outside, handing her fistfuls of clay. From inside, she increases the number of circles. Soon we see only her hands, and white wisps of smoke.

The neck on the pot narrows like an amphora. The shadow creeps over the ground. The man tests the sides. He kneads the last lump of clay, flattens it on a rock, lifts it over the pot. Her fingers reach up to receive it. Together they center the lid. From outside he seals all the edges.

Then, wiping sweat and clay from his face, he squats in the shade of the pot, watches the slant of the sun.

By sunset the clay seems dry. He begins to pile stones in a ring, higher and higher until they arch into a roof. He brings pine logs, charcoal, and twigs.

The others return to watch flames through chinks between stones.

The kiln glows all night.

By sunrise the embers are grey, the jar done.

Contributors

KATHARYN MACHAN AAL was born in Woodbury, Connecticut, in 1952. Since 1975 she has lived in Ithaca, New York, where she directed the Feminist Women's Writing Workshops and coordinated the Ithaca Community Poets. She holds a doctorate in Interpretation (Performance Studies) from Northwestern University and is on the faculty of the Writing Program of Ithaca College. Her poems have appeared in many magazines and anthologies, and she is the author of fourteen published collections, the most recent of which is *Redwing Women* (winner of the CrazyQuilt Press annual competition). §

ANYA ACHTENBERG's poetry has been published in numerous journals and magazines. Her first book, *I Know What the Small Girl Knew*, was published in 1983 by Holy Cow! Press. She has taught literature and creative writing to adults, been a poet-in-residence in Minnesota and New York, worked with teachers on developing student writing, and currently teaches writing and reading to school dropouts.

MONA ELAINE ADILMAN, a Montrealer and McGill graduate, has published four books of poetry: *Beat of Wings*, *Cult of Concrete*, *Piece Work*, and *Nighty-Knight*. Her poems have appeared in numerous anthologies including *Women on War* (Simon & Schuster) and *The Anthology of Magazine Verse & Yearbook of American Poetry*. She has edited an anthology, *Spirits of the Age: Poets of Conscience*, and a new collection of poetry, *Candles in the Dark*, is forthcoming from Mosaic Press.

DORI APPEL, a poet, playwright, and fiction writer, is also an actress and co-Artistic Director of Mixed Company Theater in Ashland, Oregon. Her plays, *Female Troubles* and *Girl Talk* (co-authored with Carolyn Myers), have toured widely, and her latest play, *Fun House Mirror*, is scheduled for production on the East Coast in 1990. Her poems and stories have appeared in many magazines and anthologies, and she is the recipient of several national awards. §

MELETA MURDOCK BAKER lives in Lebanon, Maine, with her husband, daughter, and several dozen wild birds. She is teacher at Wells High School and is advisor to the student literary magazine, *Writers' Bloc*. Her piano is dusty and her quilt is incomplete, but her poetry has been published in *Z Miscellaneous*, *The Black Fly Review*, *Women's Record*, and *The Belladonna*.

MILDRED BARKER lives in Stone Ridge, New York, where she writes for a local newspaper, the *Kingston Freeman*. She is fiction editor of *Oxalis*, a small literary magazine. She once worked in a tomato cannery in Oakland, California.

DR. CAROL BARRETT is on the graduate faculty of The Union Institute in Cincinnati, Ohio. A poet and psychologist, she has published in psychology, women's studies, and gerontology journals, as well as numerous literary magazines, including *Nimrod*, *Poet Lore*, and *Kansas Quarterly*. At one time she was a choreographer for the Mid-America Dance Company.

DENISE BERGMAN has poems published in *Sojourner, Moving Out, Pig Iron*, and others. She is editor of *City River of Voices*, a poetry anthology about urban issues. She lives in Cambridge, Massachusetts.

KATE BRAID is a journeywoman carpenter who teaches construction at the British Columbia Institute of Technology. Much of her creative and political work is around the subject of women in trades. She is a member of the Vancouver Industrial Writer's Union and has published articles and poems in several periodicals and an anthology, *East of Main*. Her most recent publication is a book of profiles of Canadian tradeswomen. She is presently writing a novel and preparing a broadcast on women in trades for CBC Radio.

KAREN BRODINE, a typesetter, found poetic inspiration at her job and in her rigorous life of political activism and leadership in the Freedom Socialist Party and Radical Women. Her award-winning work has been widely published in feminist, left, lesbian/gay, and literary journals. Her fourth book of poetry, *Woman Sitting at the Machine, Thinking*, was recently published by Red Letter Press. Brodine died of cancer in 1987 at the age of 40. §

MARY PIERCE BROSMER is a feminist poet and teacher who lives in Cincinnati, Ohio, with her son, Colin, and a richness of friends, students, and colleagues who inspire and support her work. Her poems have appeared in *Sojourner, Forum: A Women's Studies Quarterly*, and *Early Ripening*, an anthology of poems by contemporary American women.

ISABELLE BRUDER is a New Jersey poet working in New York as an editor. She has a forthcoming chapbook of poetry, *View from Here*, co-authored with her mother, Florence.

LORI BURKHALTER-LACKEY was born and educated in Los Angeles completing her photographic training at Otis/Parsons Art Institute. Her work has been exhibited in many California galleries. Her work has been featured in numerous Papier-Mache publications. §

JANET CARNCROSS CHANDLER holds an M.F.A. in Writing from Goddard and an M.S.W. from the George Warren Brown School of Social Work, Washington University in St. Louis. She was a social worker for thirty years and after retirement in 1971 took up the poet's pen. She has five published collections of poetry, the most recent of which is *Flight of the Wild Goose* (Papier-Mache Press, 1989).

MAXINE COMBS lives and teaches in Washington, DC. She has a book of poems, *Swimming Out of the Collective Unconscious* (Wineberry Press, 1989), and five of her stories won the 1989 Slough Press Fiction Prize and were published in a chapbook under the title, *The Foam of Perilous Seas.* §

BARBARA CROOKER has managed to publish 400 poems in magazines like *Yankee*, the *Christian Science Monitor, Country Journal,* and *Organic Gardening* and has received various awards for her writing. She has worked as a carhop, salesclerk, camp counselor, postal worker, tampon tester, slavic librarian, and civil service test writer. Most recently, she has been teaching part-time and staying home with her children full-time. §

KATHRYN DANIELS is a fiction writer and poet who lives in New York City. Her poetry has been published in *Dark Horse, Earth's Daughters, Korone,* and *Cat's Eye.* "Take This Job and" is her first published fiction. Another story is forthcoming in an anthology on women and body image.

TONI DE BONNEVAL, under a different name, writes business histories and articles on business and education. Her fiction is forthcoming in *Other Voices.*

SUE DORO was born in 1937 in Wisconsin where she worked as a machinist for over twelve years.   She is currently an Equal Opportunity Specialist for the Federal Department of Labor. She has authored two poetry books: *Of Birds and Factories* and *Heart, Home and Hard Hats.* Her poems have appeared in numerous magazines, journals, and anthologies, including *Women Brave in the Face of Danger* (The Crossing Press).

KATHRYN EBERLY is a poet, sometimes struggling to write fiction. She works as a clerk at the tuberculosis clinic at San Francisco General Hospital. She has work forthcoming in *Sing Heavenly Muse!* and *Word of Mouth: Short-Short Writing by Women* (The Crossing Press).

SUSAN EISENBERG is a poet/writer, parent, and union electrician in Boston. Author of the poetry book, *It's a Good Thing I'm Not Macho* (Whetstone), she has recently completed a performance video, *Coffee Break Secrets,* scripted from poetry about daily work. Her articles abut affirmative action in the construction industry have appeared in *The Nation* and *Hard-Hatted Women* (The Seal Press). She has taught poetry at University of Massachusetts at Boston.

RINA FERRARELLI is a poet and translator whose work has appeared in *Ball State University Forum, The Hudson Review, Tar River Poetry,* and *Living Inland* (Bennington Press, 1989). *Light without Motion,* her first booklength translation, is just released from Owl Creek Press. §

JEAN FLANAGAN has been published in *Connecticut River Review, Harbor Review, The Worcester Review,* and other small presses. Recently she completed compiling an anthology entitled *Back in My Body.* She lives in Arlington, Massachusetts, with her nine-year-old daughter and husband. She works at MIT in Cambridge as a communications officer in Nuclear Science.

KATHY FREEPERSON wrote, directed, and produced for the Tampa Feminist Guerrilla Theatre for ten years. Since 1979 she has lived in Gainesville, Florida, where she performs at rallies, universities, and Women's Voices events. Her work has been published in *Kalliope, Sinister Wisdom, La Bella Figura,* and numerous other journals, magazines, and collections.

DEBORAH FRUIN, who now lives in San Francisco, has worked as a magazine writer and editor on both coasts. *"Adeste Fideles"* is her second published short story.

CLYTIA FULLER specializes in photographing women, children, and the Southwest. Her photographs have appeared in *Women's Spirit, Plexus, Erotic by Nature,* and other publications. She lives in Santa Cruz, California, where her work has received local awards.

ELLEN GRUBER GARVEY teaches and is completing work on her doctorate in the English department at the University of Pennsylvania. Her writing has appeared in *Feminist Studies, The Minnesota Review,* and in the anthologies *Speaking for Myself* and *Word of Mouth: Short-Short Writings by Women.*

PENNY GASAWAY is a native Californian who received her B.A. from California State University, San Bernardino, and her M.F.A. from UC Irvine. She has been published in *The Pacific Review* and *Porter Gulch Review.* She is currently working on a collection of poems entitled *China.* She resides with her husband in Santa Cruz, California. The body of her work is derived from her life experience in South Central Los Angeles.

ELIZABETH GILLILAND is an artist and writer who lives in Manhattan. She holds an M.F.A. in studio art and is working on a second master's degree in social work. Publications include *The Nation, The Saturday Review, Southern Poetry Review,* and *Kalliope,* for which she is a contributing editor. Her art has been exhibited in New York and in Florida, where she grew up. Her interview of artist Louise Fishman in the Winter 1989 issue of *Kalliope* has been nominated for a Pushcart Prize.

BINA GOLDFIELD has published in Andrew Mountain Press, *Slant, Bitterroot,* and the *New York Times*. She has authored a feminist handbook and is a member of the Poetry Society of America. She resides in New York City. §

MARIANNE GONTARZ, a resident of Marin County, California, is a gerontological social worker and a professional photographer whose work has appeared in numerous publications including *Ourselves Growing Older*.

VICTORIA HAMLIN lives in Oakland, California, and is both an artist and a sheet metal worker. She studied art at City College of New York and one of her paintings was awarded first prize at the National California Arts Competition in Sacramento.

HOLLY HILDEBRAND has published her poetry and fiction in such literary magazines as *Birmingham Poetry Review, Thema, Stone Drum,* and *Fishes Magazine*. A native of St. Louis, she received a B.A. from Southern Illinois University at Edwardsville and an M.S. from the University of Illinois. She now lives in Houston, Texas, where she is a freelance writer and an editor on the Universal Desk of the *Houston Post*.

JANE ELLEN IBUR lives in South St. Louis. Her work has appeared in *Webster Review* and the first *Anthology of Missouri Women Writers* and is forthcoming in the anthology *Giving Birth to Ourselves*. She designs an original line of humor survivalist jewelry for the water retentive woman.

RUTH HARRIET JACOBS is a sociologist, gerontologist, and advocate for women. She has authored five books, including *Older Women, Surviving and Thriving* (Family Service America) and *Button, Button, Who Has the Button?* (Crones' Own Press). She is a researcher at the Wellesley College Center for Research on Women and teaches at other Massachusetts colleges. She speaks throughout the country on women and aging and founded Remarkable Aging Smart People (RASP). §

SUSAN JACOBSON attended Bryn Mawr College. She was a poet-in-residence for the Writer's Conference at Edinboro University of Pennsylvania for four years and poet-in-residence at Western Pennsylvania School for the Deaf for three years. Since 1986 she has been a poet-in-the-classroom for the Pittsburgh area schools. She works on an orthopedic unit of a Pittsburgh hospital and trauma center. §

NANCY ROXBURY KNUTSON was born in Tucson, Arizona, and now lives in Plantation, Florida, with her husband and two daughters. Her poems have appeared in many magazines, including the *American Poetry Review*. Her chapbook, *Nothing Should Fall to Waste*, won the Artist's Wreath Award judged by Denise Levertov. She is a MacDowell Colony Fellow and won the 1982 Berkeley Poets Cooperative Award.

CANDIDA LAWRENCE was born in Berkeley, California, and has lived in Europe, on the East Coast, and now in Santa Cruz, California. She has been a mother, a teacher, an editor, and a writer. Her work has appeared in *The Missouri Review, Ohio Journal, Passages North, Moving Out*, and other publications.

DIANE LEFER has published more than two dozen stories in magazines and journals, including *The Agni Review, Boulevard, Playgirl*, and *Redbook*. A five-time winner in PEN Syndicated Fiction competitions, she's also received grants from the National Endowment for the Arts and the New York Foundation for the Arts. She teaches in the M.F.A. in Writing program at Vermont College.

KAREN LOEB lived in Florida for a number of years, prior to teaching at the University of Wisconsin, Eau Claire. Two of her stories have received PEN Syndicated Fiction Awards, and her writing has appeared in many magazines and newspapers. Recent stories have appeared in *South Dakota Review*, the *Orlando Sentinel*, and *Korone 5 & 6*.

JOAN MAIERS teaches writing at Marylhurst College near Portland, Oregon. She has presented her poetry at the Bumbershoot Arts Festival, Seattle, and at ArtQuake, Portland. She was invited to read her sequence of poems, "Lives in the Balance," at the 1988 NWWSA conference at Portland State University and at the Eighth Annual Gender Studies Symposium, Lewis and Clark College. Her recent poems appear in *The Bellingham Review, The Other Side*, and *Hubbub*.

EILEEN MALONE lives in the San Francisco Bay Area where she teaches off-campus at senior centers for a California community college. Her writing workshops utilize the creative process as therapy. Her work has appeared in over 200 publications nationally and she is now being published in the United Kingdom. §

DORIS VANDERLIPP MANLEY is a resident of Cherry Valley, New York. "Lest my poem, 'On Being a Bureaucrat in Spring', leave the wrong impression, I hasten to add that, on the whole, going back into the job world at the age of 43 helped me to grow. Poetry continued to be my vehicle for coming to grips with turbulent experiences. While formerly I had written on top of the washing machine, now I wrote while commuting or in the middle of the night." §

MOLLY MARTIN is an electrician and a feminist activist. She is editor of *Tradeswomen Magazine* and author of *Hard-Hatted Women: Stories of Struggle and Success in the Trades.* She is a founder of Tradeswomen, Inc., a national grassroots organization of women in nontraditional blue collar work. She also serves on the Board of Equal Rights Advocates, a public interest law firm, and the San Francisco Commission on the Status of Women. She lives in San Francisco and works for the city water department.

LILLIAN MORRISON is the author of fourteen books: six collections of her own poems, six collections of folk rhymes for children, and two anthologies, *Sprints and Distances* and *Rhythm Road: Poems to Move To.* Her poetry has appeared in periodicals such as *Confrontation, Images,* and *Poets On:,* and in many anthologies. §

VIRGINIA RUDASILL MORTENSON, a life-long resident of Des Moines, Iowa, and graduate of Drake University, devoted twenty years to teaching English, raising a family, and "making excuses for not writing." In the past five years, with sons flown from the nest and a switch to a counseling position, she no longer has excuses and has written two-and-a-half novels, two-and-a-half short story collections, and fifty poems.

LESLÉA NEWMAN received a 1989 Massachusetts Artists Fellowship for Poetry. She edited *Bubbe Meisehs by Shayneh Maidelehs: An Anthology of Poetry by Jewish Granddaughters about Our Grandmothers.* She has published seven books; the newest ones include a children's book, *Heather Has Two Mommies,* and a short story collection entitled *Secrets.*

GINNY ODENBACH lives in Wright, Wyoming, where she teaches gifted students at Cottonwood Elementary and Wright Jr-Sr High School. She has an M.S. in Education/Administration. Her poetry has been published in *Wyoming Rural Electric News, Westering, Wyoming Writing 1988 and 1989,* and *Plainswoman.* Coming to Wyoming from Nebraska, Ginny has lived in Wright for the past nine years.

RHONDA OXLEY, a previous resident of Oregon and Los Angeles, now resides in Santa Cruz where she attempts to capture "a nice yin yang energy in body and photo art."

JACKLYN POTTER grew up singing songs, with her father accompanying her on the banjo or piano. She sang on TV and radio, at Kiwanis Club banquets, Virginia country hoe-downs, and at Red Cross Hospitals for wounded veterans, with Bob Hope's USO show. She holds degrees in Literature and Creative Writing. She has been a teacher, a county 4-H agent, and an organizer for migrant farmworkers. Her articles, reviews, and poems have appeared in numerous publications, including the *Eastern Shore News, Poets On: Working, Plainsong,* and *Poets Lore.*

BONNIE MICHAEL PRATT is a freelance writer and poet living in Winston-Salem, North Carolina. Her special interests are women's issues and metaphysics. She has published in many literary magazines as well as commercial magazines and has been included in several anthologies. §

BERNICE RENDRICK lives and writes in Scotts Valley, California. Her interests include poetry, the environment, family, and friends. She has published in *Porter Gulch Review, Plainswoman, Coydog Review,* and *Quarry West.*

GEORGEANN ESKIEVICH RETTBERG teaches kindergarten and a fourth and fifth grade poetry workshop for the Pittsburgh Public Schools. Her first chapbook, *Steelworker's Family,* was published by M.A.F. Press in 1989. Her second chapbook is forthcoming from Naked Man Press.

SUSANNA RICH holds a Ph.D. from New York University specializing in theories of the creative process. Her thesis, "Mirror, Mirror: The Stepmother's Cinderella," is an autobiographical study of the process by which she wrote her first novel. She is currently an Assistant Professor of English at Kean College of New Jersey. Her popular workshop, "Writer's Block Busting," is featured at the annual Trenton State Writer's Conference. Her work has appeared in *Et Cetera, Ailanthus, West Branch,* and *Humor.*

ELISAVIETTA RITCHIE's seven collections include *Tightening the Circle over Eel Country,* winner of the Great Lakes Colleges Association's New Writer's Award for Best First Book of Poetry, 1975-76, and *Raking the Snow,* winner of the 1981 Washington Writers Publishing House competition. Three of her stories were PEN Syndicated Fiction winners. Publications include *Poetry,* the *American Scholar,* the *Christian Science Monitor,* and the *New York Times.* She edited *The Dolphin's Arc: Poems on Endangered Creature of the Sea.* She writes and teaches in Washington, DC. §

RUTHANN ROBSON recently moved from Florida to California where she is working on a nonfiction book, *Lesbian Law.* "For Love or Money" is part of a collection of interrelated stories, *Cecile,* to be published by Firebrand Books in 1991. Her short story collection, *Eye of a Hurricane,* is currently available from Firebrand.

SAVINA A. ROXAS is a freelance writer who holds an M.F.A. and Ph.D. from the University of Pittsburgh. She is a former professor at Clarion State University. Her poetry and fiction have appeared in *The Antigonish Review, The Black Fly Review, Amelia/Cicada*, and *Modern Haiku*. §

LORRAINE SCHEIN is a New York poet and science fiction writer. Her poetry and fiction has appeared in *Heresies* and *The New York Quarterly*, among others, and more recently in *Semiotext(e) SF* and *Memories and Visions* (The Crossing Press). She has been unemployed many times.

JOANNE SELTZER has authored three chapbooks: *Adirondack Lake Poems* (Loft Press, 1985), *Suburban Landscape* (M.A.F. Press, 1988), and *Inside Invisible Walls* (Bard Press, 1989). Her poems have appeared widely in literary magazines and anthologies, including *When I Am an Old Woman I Shall Wear Purple*. She has also published short fiction, literary essays, and translations of French poetry. §

CATHERINE SHAW's poetry has appeared in various publications, including *Rhino, Pig Iron, The Glens Falls Review*, and *Matrix Women's Newsmagazine*. She offers "Off Duty" as a tribute to the overextended woman of today. §

ENID SHOMER is the author of *Stalking the Florida Panther*, which won The Word Works' book prize. Her poems appear in *Poetry, Ploughshares, Tikkun, New Letters*, and others. She has received fellowships for the National Endowment for the Arts and the Florida Arts Council. Her poetry is the subject of one episode of "The Poet & the Poem," a syndicated public radio series chosen for broadcast worldwide by the "Voice of America." §

ELAINE STARKMAN teaches Short Story Writing for University of California, Berkeley Extension. Her own work keeps evolving with her life and age. She has written both prose and poetry, her prose appearing in such national publications as *Between Ourselves: Letters between Mothers & Daughters* (Houghton Miffin, 1983). She recently co-edited *Without a Single Answer: Poems of Contemporary Israel* (Judah Magnes Press, 1990). She also studies tai chi in Walnut Creek, California, where she lives.

PATTI TANA is Professor of English in the SUNY system and Associate Editor of the *Long Island Quarterly*. She participated in the production and performance of an album of women's work songs, *The Work of the Women*, and is the author of two books of poetry, *How Odd This Ritual of Harmony* and *Ask the Dreamer Where Night Begins*. §

RANDEANE TETU has received several national awards for fiction. A resident of Haddam, Connecticut, her work appears in *The Massachusetts Review, Loonfeather, The Fiddlehead,* and other magazines. She has written two collections of short stories and is working on her third novel. §

SANDY THACKER is staff photographer for *Tradeswomen* magazine. Her photographs have been exhibited internationally and have appeared in many publications. Her photographs were also part of the "Women Artists at Work" exhibit at the Eye Gallery in San Francisco.

BARBARA UNGER has published four books of poetry and her fiction collection *Dying for Uncle Ray and Other Stories* is due in 1990 from Kendall-Hunt. Her fiction has appeared in *Midstream, American Fiction,* and *Jewish Currents,* among others. She teaches English and creative writing at Rockland Community College where she is a Professor of English. She is working on a literary anthology of writers from the Bronx, and a novel.

DEBRA RIGGIN WAUGH lives with her dog and two cats in Takoma Park, Maryland, and works as a senior writer/editor for a consulting firm. Her work has appeared in anthologies and journals, including *Deviance* and *The Takoma Voice.*

MICHELE WOLF's poems have appeared in *Boulevard, The Hudson Review, The Greenfield Review,* and elsewhere. A New York-based magazine writer, she was National Arts Club Scholar in Poetry at the Bread Loaf Writers' Conference in 1987 and has received residency fellowships from the Edward F. Albee Foundation, the Virginia Center for the Creative Arts, and the Helene Wurlitzer Foundation of New Mexico. §

§Denotes contributors whose work has appeared in previous Papier-Mache Press anthologies. To receive information about other Papier-Mache Press books or other books available from the above writers, please send a self-addressed stamped envelope to: Papier-Mache Press, 795 Via Manzana, Watsonville, CA 95076.